HOW TO LIVE & WOF

In this Series

How to Apply for a Job
How to Apply to an Industrial Tribunal
How to Be a Freelance Secretary
How to Be a Freelance Journalist
How to Be a Local Councillor
How to Be an Effective School Governor
How to Become an Au Pair
How to Buy & Run a Shop
How to Buy & Run a Small Hotel
How to Choose a Private School
How to Claim State Benefits
How to Communicate at Work
How to Conduct Staff Appraisals
How to Counsel People at Work
How to Do Voluntary Work Abroad
How to Do Your Own Advertising
How to Do Your Own PR
How to Emigrate
How to Employ & Manage Staff
How to Enjoy Retirement
How to Find Temporary Work Abroad
How to Get a Job Abroad
How to Get a Job in America
How to Get a Job in Australia
How to Get a Job in Europe
How to Get a Job in France
How to Get a Job in Germany
How to Get a Job in Hotels & Catering
How to Get a Job in Travel & Tourism
How to Get Into Films & TV
How to Get Into Radio
How to Get That Job
How to Help Your Child at School
How to Invest in Stocks & Shares
How to Keep Business Accounts
How to Know Your Rights at Work
How to Know Your Rights: Students
How to Know Your Rights: Teachers
How to Live & Work in America
How to Live & Work in Australia
How to Live & Work in Belgium
How to Live & Work in France
How to Live & Work in Germany
How to Live & Work in the Gulf
How to Live & Work in Hong Kong
How to Live & Work in Italy
How to Live & Work in Japan
How to Live & Work in New Zealand
How to Live & Work in Portugal
How to Live & Work in Saudi Arabia
How to Live & Work in Spain
How to Lose Weight & Keep Fit
How to Make a Wedding Speech
How to Manage a Sales Team
How to Manage Budgets & Cash Flows
How to Manage Computers at Work
How to Manage People at Work
How to Manage Your Career
How to Master Book-Keeping
How to Master Business English
How to Master GCSE Accounts
How to Master Languages
How to Master Public Speaking
How to Pass Exams Without Anxiety
How to Pass That Interview
How to Plan a Wedding
How to Prepare Your Child for School
How to Publish a Book
How to Publish a Newsletter
How to Raise Business Finance
How to Raise Funds & Sponsorship
How to Rent & Buy Property in France
How to Rent & Buy Property in Italy
How to Retire Abroad
How to Return to Work
How to Run a Local Campaign
How to Run a Voluntary Group
How to Sell Your Business
How to Spend a Year Abroad
How to Start a Business from Home
How to Start a New Career
How to Start Wordprocessing
How to Study Abroad
How to Study and Learn
How to Study & Live in Britain
How to Survive at College
How to Survive Divorce
How to Take Care of Your Heart
How to Teach Abroad
How to Travel Round the World
How to Understand Finance at Work
How to Use a Library
How to Work from Home
How to Work in an Office
How to Work with Dogs
How to Write a Press Release
How to Write a Report
How to Write an Assignment
How to Write an Essay
How to Write Business Letters
How to Write for Publication
How to Write for Television

Other titles in preparation

LIVE & WORK
IN GERMANY

A handbook for short and longstay visitors

Christine Hall

Second Edition

How To Books

Other titles by the same author
How to Get a Job in Germany
How to Be a Freelance Journalist
Living and Working in China (in preparation)

British Library Cataloguing in Publication Data
A catalogue record for this book is available from the British Library.

© Copyright 1995 by Christine Hall.

Published in 1995 by How To Books Ltd, Plymbridge House, Estover Road, Plymouth PL6 7PZ, United Kingdom. Tel: Plymouth (01752) 735251/ 695745. Fax: (01752) 695699. Telex: 45635.

First published in 1991
Second edition (rewritten) 1995

Note: The material contained in this book is set out in good faith for general guidance and no liability can be accepted for loss or expense incurred as a result of relying in particular circumstances on statements made in the book. The law and regulations are complex and liable to change, and readers should check the current position with the relevant authorities before making personal arrangements.

Typeset by Concept Communications (Design & Print) Ltd, Crayford, Kent. Printed and bound by The Cromwell Press, Broughton Gifford, Melksham, Wiltshire

Contents

Preface   9

List of illustrations   10

1   Introducing Germany   11

     Going to Germany   11
     Foreigners in Germany   11
     German politics   13
     Looking at the geography   17
     The climate   23
     Practising your religion   23
     Case studies   23

2   Looking at the economy   25

     Comparing East and West   25
     Germany's top twelve   26
     Sectors of the economy   27
     Useful addresses   34

3   Understanding the Germans   35

     Building links with Germany   35
     The Anglo-German Association   35
     The Anglo-German Club   35
     The Goethe-Institut   36
     Exploring Germany in your holidays   36
     Different attitudes   38
     Case studies   46

4   Learning the language   48

     Studying German before you go   48

	Studying German in Germany	48
	German for special purposes	49
	Language courses with work experience	50
	Joining a university summer school	51
	Learning at a Goethe-Institut	53
	Booking through CESA	53
	Case studies	54
	Useful addresses	55
	Checklist	56
5	Finding a job	57
	Looking at the employment situation	57
	Using the state employment service	57
	Using employment agencies	59
	Avoiding pitfalls	59
	Looking at newspaper advertisements	60
	Placing your own advertisements	61
	Writing your application letter	63
	Writing a German-style CV	66
	What to translate	66
	Voluntary and au pair work	67
	Temp and vacation jobs	69
	Case studies	69
	Useful words and phrases	70
6	Handling the paperwork	73
	Visas, residence and work permits	73
	Registration	74
	Residence permits	75
	Social security, health and insurance	75
	Paying taxes	78
	Banking	78
	Useful words and phrases	79
	Checklist	80
7	Finding accommodation	81
	Flat-hunting	81
	Buying a place	86
	Furnishing your flat	86
	Buying household equipment	87
	Case study	88
	Addresses	88
	Useful words and phrases	88

8	Working in Germany	90
	Signing your contract	90
	Getting paid	90
	Joining a trade union	91
	Hours of work	93
	Handing in your notice	93
	Annual leave	93
	How to get on with colleagues	93
	Case studies	94
	Useful words and phrases	95
9	Living in Germany	96
	Shopping in Germany	96
	Making friends	102
	Practising your hobbies	103
	Cooking and baking	104
	Going out	107
	Visiting someone's home	112
	Entertaining at home	112
	Looking at customs, traditions and holidays	113
	German newspapers and magazines	115
	Case studies	119
	Useful words and phrases	120
10	Education and training	122
	Finding the right school for your child	122
	Universities and polytechnics	127
	Private colleges	128
	Vocational training	129
	Adult education	130
	Correspondence courses	130
	Useful words and phrases	131
11	Being green	132
	Problems in the East	132
	Travelling and commuting	132
	Waste management	135
	'Green Dots' and 'Blue Angels'	137
	How to be green	137
	Case studies	138
	Useful words and phrases	139

12   Communicating and doing business   140

       Conversation   140
       Making a phone call   140
       Writing a letter   143
       At the post office   146
       Punctuality   149
       Starting a business   149
       Chambers of commerce   150
       Trade fairs   151
       Useful contacts for business people   152
       Useful words and phrases   154

Further reading   156

Glossary of German terms   161

Useful addresses   163

Index   175

Preface

Many thanks to everyone who helped me with this book. Special thanks to my friends Evelyn Thomsen and Hans Christoph Neidlein, my sister-in-law Petra Lauhöfer Sterk and my brother Jürgen Sterk who helped with the research; writer Claire Gill, who proof-read several chapters; Sarah Cross for her detailed report about her time in Germany; Peter Adams of the Heusenstamm and Tonbridge Friendship Circle for his advice; Nick Phillips for his continued support of the project; Joe Parr of the British Chamber of Commerce for the contacts; the German Embassy in London for the wealth of material provided; Hansgerd Schomacher of Kapito, Madeleine Kötter of DID and Martin Mayer of Horizonte for the interviews, and everyone else for their contributions large and small. Also, in grateful memory to my grandparents Elisabeth Dilger Hall and Thomas Hall for their kindness and support.

The sample letters in this book use fictititious names and addresses; I created most of the illustrations using PageMaker and CorelDraw software and clipart. Some of the recipes were supplied by my German friends, others are extracts from *A Little German Cookbook*, published with the kind permission of Appletree.

If you are going to live in Germany, I would like to hear from you. Your experiences, comments and suggestions will be valuable for future editions of this book. Contact me c/o How To Books Ltd, Plymbridge House, Estover Road, Plymouth PL6 7PZ, UK.

Christine Hall

List of Illustrations

1. Germany and her neighbours   14

2. German Bundesländer   22

3. Sample 'situations vacant' advertisement
    with translation   62

4. Sample application letter with translation   64

5. 'Accommodation vacant' advertisements
    with translation   82

6. 'Accommodation wanted' advertisements
    with translation   84

7. Shopping list   98

8. Looking at a German menu   110

9. German magazines   118

10. Sample business letter with translation   144

1
Introducing Germany

GOING TO GERMANY

Since the 1950s, Germany has attracted job-hunters from many other countries. Some come because of the political stability, others because of the social security network, which is probably the most comprehensive in the world. High wages and a high living standard also play a role. For example, most Germans can afford to live comfortably, own a car, and go on a holiday abroad at least once a year.

High technical standards encourage foreign nationals to gain work experience in Germany; others spend a year or so as an au pair or at a university to learn the language and widen their horizon.

For many years, it was fairly easy to get jobs in Germany; the government invited workers from abroad to fill the vacancies. This situation has changed.

Germany still offers a high living standard, good social security, political stability and high technical standards. But like all western countries, Germany's economy has suffered a setback during the recession. Unification has made matters worse, and it will take several years until Germany recovers from the impact.

East Germans and many refugees from other countries compete for job vacancies as well as accommodation. It would be naive to assume that Germany is the promised land where you can get a well-paid job without speaking the language, without experience and qualifications, or without hard work.

However, if you are prepared to learn the language and have realistic expectations, you can find a job, develop a career, settle down, make friends, and feel welcome in Germany.

FOREIGNERS IN GERMANY

1951–1956   With the *Wirtschaftswunder* (economic miracle), Ger-

many's gross national product increases by 9.5 per cent a year.

1955   The creation of the German army takes about 500,000 men out of the labour market. Germany needs more workers urgently. The German and Italian governments agree on recruiting Italians to fill German vacancies.

1957–1958   There are more job vacancies than applicants in Germany.

1957–1967   The working week is reduced from 46.1 to 41.6 hours.

1960   The German economy is 410,000 workers short. The government hopes that 100,000 workers will come from East Germany, and plans to recruit another 100,000 workers from other countries.

1960–1972   The number of gainfully employed Germans is reduced by 2.3 million, mostly because of low birth rates in the post-war period.

1961   The Berlin Wall is built. This stops the influx of refugees from East Germany. The German and Turkish governments agree on recruiting Turkish workers for Germany.

1963   The German and Moroccan governments sign a similar accord.

1964   Germany starts recruiting workers from Portugal.

1965   Germany starts recruiting workers from Tunisia.

1966–1967   More than one million foreign nationals work in Germany.

1967   The first post-war recession leads to a decline in employment of foreigners.

1968   Germany still needs more workers and starts recruiting in Yugoslavia.

1973   Now 2.6 million foreign nationals are employed in Germany, and they have 1.8 million family members living with them. The oil crisis results in a global recession, and Germany stops foreign recruitment.

Since 1993   The number of foreign nationals in Germany continues to increase despite the foreign recruitment stop. This is because of foreigners joining their families in Germany and because of the high birth rate among foreigners in Germany.

1978   Because of the high number of foreign nationals in Germany, the government appoints a representative for integrating foreign employees and their families.

Since 1989   The Berlin Wall comes down. At the same time, the radical changes in Eastern Europe bring an influx of ethnic Germans into Germany.

Today   About 6.2 million foreign nationals live in Germany. Of these, only 2.9 million are gainfully employed. It is fairly easy for members of European Union member states to go job-hunting in Germany, but few vacancies are available. Only applicants with particular skills – for example, qualified nursing staff and construction workers – are encouraged.

GERMAN POLITICS

The German constitution is based on the **Grundgesetz** (basic law), which was adopted in 1949. It was meant as a temporary measure, but has proved to be a solid, working foundation for democracy.

The classical freedoms embodied in the Grundgesetz include: the freedom of religion, speech and press, arts and scholarship, the guarantee of property, the right to form coalitions, the right to privacy of the home, of mail and of telecommunications, the right to conscientious objection to enforced military service, and protection from enforced labour.

The Grundgesetz also includes the rights of equality: nobody may be discriminated against because of their origin, race, language, sex, convictions, religion or political views. In practice, for many years there

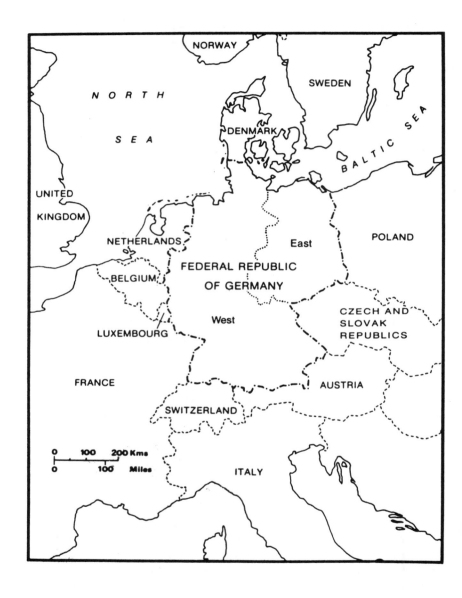

Fig. 1. Germany and her neighbours.

were some German laws which contradicted the equality of sexes. For a long time, men had the final word in the upbringing of children, for example. And until recently women were not allowed to keep their own name if their husband objected. These matters have now been put right.

One basic right guaranteed by the Grundgesetz is the right of political asylum for foreigners persecuted on political grounds. This right had to be adapted after the influx over the years of hundreds of thousands of refugees which were more than the German economy could absorb.

The German constitution is based on five principles:

1.   Germany is a republic.

2.   Germany is a democracy.

3.   Germany is a federal state.

4.   The state is based on the rule of law.

5.   It is based on social justice.

Constitutional bodies

The head of state is not, as many foreigners assume, the Bundeskanzler, but the **Bundespräsident** (federal president). He represents the Federal Republic in its international relations and concludes agreements with foreign states. He is elected by the Federal Convention, and nominates a candidate for the office of Bundeskanzler.

The **Bundestag** is the parliamentary assembly which represents the people. It is elected by the people every four years. Its main function is to pass laws, to elect the Bundeskanzler, and to keep check on the government.

The **Bundesrat** (federal council) represents the Länder (federal states). It participates in federal legislation. It consists not of elected representatives of the people but of members of the Länder governments.

The **Bundesregierung** (federal government) consists of the Bundeskanzler who is the chairperson and head of government, and the federal ministers.

The **Bundeskanzler** chooses the ministers and proposes them to the Bundespräsident. He or she also decides the number of ministers and their areas of responsibility.

The **Bundesgerichtshof** (federal constitutional court) is based in Karsruhe and is the guardian of the Grundgesetz. For example, it rules on disputes between the federal government and the federal states. It can declare that a party poses a threat to freedom and democracy and can order the party's dissolution. Every citizen has the right to appeal to the Bundesgerichtshof if they feel their basic rights have been violated by the state.

Parties in the Bundestag

The major German parties are:

- **BÜNDNIS 90/DIE GRÜNEN** – merger of the green party with the alliance party (which emerged from the civil rights movement which in 1989-90 brought about the peaceful revolution in the former GDR).

- **CDU (Christlich-Demokratische Union)** – conservative party.

- **CSU (Christlich-Soziale Union)** – Bavarian equivalent of CSU.

- **FDP (Freie Demokratische Partei)** – liberal party.

- **PDS (Partei des Demokratischen Sozialisten)** – the successor of the former Socialist Unity Party (SED) in East Germany.

- **SPD (Sozialdemokratische Partei Deutschlands)** – socialist party.

No party can be represented in the Bundestag unless it gains at least 5 per cent of all votes, or at least three constituency seats. This is to prevent tiny parties from entering the parliament (which happened in the period of the Weimar Republic with disastrous results).

Addresses
Bündnis 90/Die Grünen, Colmantstr. 36, D-53115 Bonn, Germany.

Christlich Demokratische Union Deutschlands (CDU), Konrad-Adenauer-Haus, Friedrich-Ebert-Allee 73–75, D-53113 Bonn, Germany.

Christlich-Soziale Union in Bayern (CSU), Nymphenburger Str. 64–66, D-80335 München, Germany.

Freie Demokratische Partei (FDP), Thomas-Dehler-Haus, Baunscheidtstr. 15, D-53113 Bonn, Germany.

Partei des Demokratischen Sozialisten (PDS), Bundeshaus, Görrestr. 15, D-58113 Bonn, Germany.

Sozialdemokratische Partei Deutschlands (SPD), Erich-Ollenhauer-Haus, Ollenhauerstr. 1, D-53113 Bonn, Germany.

LOOKING AT THE GEOGRAPHY

Western Germany consists of the Northern Plain, the Central Uplands and the Bavarian Alps in the South. Eastern Germany has plains and rolling hills in the north, Central Highlands and the Erzgebirge Mountains further south.

Berlin is the capital for ceremonial purposes, Bonn for administration.

The Federal Republic of Germany consists of sixteen Länder (states). They are independent in many matters of cultural development, nature conservation, arts, education, landscape and water management.

Baden-Württemberg

Situation: south-west.
Population: 10 million.
Area: 35,751 square kilometres.
Capital: Stuttgart.
Other major towns: Mannheim, Ulm, Freiburg, Konstanz, Karlsruhe.
Scenic features: Schwarzwald (Black Forest), Bodensee (Lake Constance, the second largest lake in Europe), rivers Rhein (Rhine) and Donau (Danube).
Agriculture: fruit (especially apples), wine (mostly dry), asparagus, tobacco.
Industry: precision engineering, automotive industry (including Daimler Benz, Porsche), oil refineries (especially in Karlsruhe), printing machines (Heidelberg), extensive service industries (Freiburg and Ulm), tourism.

Bayern (Bavaria)

Situation: south-east.
Population: 11.8 million
Area: 70,554 square kilometres.
Capital: München (Munich).
Other major towns: Nürnberg (Nuremberg), Fürth, Erlangen, Augsburg, Regensburg.
Scenic features: the Alps (including Germany's highest mountain, the Zugspitze) and the alpine foothills, the river Donau (Danube).

Agriculture: extensive, especially in the Alps and alpine foothills.

Industry: engineering, electrical and toy industries (including Siemens, Quelle, Grundig), automobile manufacture (including BMW, Audi), glass and porcelain factories (including Rosenthal, Hutschenreuther), breweries, tourism.

Berlin

Situation: east.
Population: 3.4 million.
Area: 889 square kilometres.
Capital: Berlin.
Industry: engineering, food and beverages, pharmaceuticals, textiles, electrical goods (including Siemens, AEG).

Brandenburg

Situation: east
Population: 2.5 million.
Area: 29,053 square kilometres.
Capital: Potsdam.
Other major towns: Eisenhüttenstadt, Cottbus, Frankfurt an der Oder.
Scenic features and regions: rugged landscape with many forests and lakes.
Agriculture: forestry (mainly fir), rye, wheat, oil-seed, potatoes, sugar-beet, fruit and vegetables.
Industry: steel (in Eisenhüttenstadt), chemical industry (Cottbus).

Bremen

Situation: north-west.
Population: 684,000
Area: 404 square kilometres.
Capital: Bremen.
Industry: transport (especially container traffic), food and beverages, aerospace, shipbuilding, maritime trading.

Hamburg

Situation: north.
Population: 1.7 million.
Area: 755 square kilometres.
Capital: Hamburg.
Industry: Germany's most important seaport and largest overseas trade centre, media industries.

Hessen (Hesse)

Situation: central.

Population: 5.9 million.

Area: 21,114 square kilometres.

Capital: Wiesbaden.

Other major towns: Darmstadt, Offenbach, Frankfurt am Main, Marburg, Giessen, Wetzler, Kassel.

Scenic features: rivers Rhein (Rhine) and Main, Bergstrasse, Taunus.

Agriculture: fruit and wine.

Industry: financial services and headquarters of the national bank Bundesbank (in Frankfurt), Europe's second largest passenger airport (in Frankfurt), machinery, locomotives, automobiles (around Kassel), optical instruments (in Wetzlar).

Mecklenburg–Westpommern (Mecklenburg–Western Pomerania)

Situation: north-east.

Population: 1.89 million.

Area: 23,598 square kilometres.

Capital: Schwerin.

Other major towns: Stralsund, Wismar, Greifswald, Rostock.

Scenic features: Baltic Sea, many lakes (including the Müritz), nature reserves.

Agriculture: fields, woods, livestock enclosures.

Industry: fishing, shipbuilding, tourism.

Niedersachsen (Lower Saxony)

Situation: north-west.

Population: 7.5 million.

Area: 47,364 square kilometres.

Capital: Hannover (Hanover).

Other major towns: Oldenburg, Goslar, Lüneburg, Salzgitter, Emden, Wolfsburg, Göttingen.

Scenic features: Harz, Weserbergland (Weser Highlands), Lüneburger Heide (heathland), North Sea marshlands, Ostfriesische Inseln (East Frisian Islands).

Agriculture: large farming area, bacon and honey.

Industry: car manufacture (including VW in Wolfsburg), silver mining (in Goslar), iron-ore mining (in Salzgitter), container vessels (Emden), communication technology (in Hannover).

Nordrhein-Westfalen (North Rhine Westfalia)

Situation: west.

Population: 17.7 million.

Area: 34,071 square kilometres.

Capital: Düsseldorf.

Other major towns: Dortmund, Duisburg, Köln (Cologne), Essen, Duisburg, Bochum, Wuppertal, Bielefeld, Leverkusen, Aachen, Bonn.

Scenic features: Former industrial landscapes and open mining areas are being turned into green areas.

Agriculture: animal husbandry, horse breeding.

Industry: the Ruhrgebiet (Ruhr District) is Europe's largest industrial area, and Germany's main source of energy; Duisburg has the largest inland port in the world; breweries (in Dortmund).

Rheinland-Pfalz (Rhineland Palatinate)

Situation: west.

Population: 3.8 million.

Area: 19,846 square kilometres.

Capital: Mainz.

Other major towns: Ludwigshafen, Idar-Oberstein, Kaiserslautern, Trier, Worms.

Scenic features: Rivers Rhein, Ahr and Mosel.

Agriculture: vineyards along the rivers, extensive forestry.

Industry: chemical (including BASF in Ludwigshafen), Germany's largest TV and radio network (ZDF in Mainz).

Saarland

Situation: west.

Population: 1.1 million.

Area: 2,570 square kilometres.

Capital: Saarbrücken.

Other major towns: Neunkirchen, Saarlouis.

Scenic features: River Saar, Hunsrück (forested Central Uplands).

Agriculture: wine.

Industry: automobile, steel, food and electronics (all concentrated in Saarbrücken), glass and ceramics (including Villeroy & Boch).

Sachsen (Saxony)

Situation: east.

Population: 4.7 million.

Area: 18,338 square kilometres.

Capital: Dresden.
Other major towns: Leipzig, Meissen, Zwickau, Chemnitz.
Scenic features: Elbe Sandstone Mountains, Erzgebirge Mountains.
Industry: porcelain (in Meissen), mechanical engineering and micro-electronics (both in Chemnitz), car manufacturing (in Zwickau), publishing (in Meissen).

Sachsen-Anhalt (Saxony-Anhalt)

Situation: north-east.
Population: 2.82 million.
Area: 20,443 square kilometres.
Capital: Magdeburg.
Other major towns: Dessau, Halle, Bitterfeld, Leuna, Wolfen, Merseburg.
Scenic features: Harz Mountains including the Brocken and the Blocksberg.
Agriculture: wheat, sugarbeet, vegetables.
Industry: sugar processing, chemical industry, lignite mining.

Schleswig-Holstein

Situation: north.
Population: 2.6 million.
Area: 15,731 square kilometres.
Capital: Kiel
Other major towns: Lübeck, Flensburg.
Scenic features: North Sea, Nordfriesische Inseln (North Frisian Islands).
Agriculture: livestock farming (especially in the marshlands along the western coast).
Industry: shipbuilding including special vessels.

Thüringen (Thuringia)

Situation: central.
Population: 2.57 million.
Area: 16,251 square kilometres.
Capital: Erfurt.
Other major towns: Jena, Gera, Weimar.
Scenic features: large forests.
Agriculture: barley, wheat, potatoes, sugarbeet, fruit.
Industry: precision and optical instruments (in Jena), car manufacture (in Eisenach).

Fig. 2. German Bundesländer.

THE CLIMATE

The German climate is mild and temperate, with an average temperature of 22 degrees Celsius in summer, and winter temperatures of between 0 and -12 degrees Celsius. Especially in the mountains, there can be much snow in the winter months. Most of the time, the climate is similar to that of other central and western European countries.

PRACTISING YOUR RELIGION

Over 58 million people in Germany belong to a Christian church. About 30 million of them are Protestants, and 28 million are Roman Catholics. The churches and the state co-operate closely. For example, most of the clergy train at state university, and the state collects the church taxes. The churches run some hospitals, nursing homes, schools and training centres. Sometimes they run local women's groups.

Church services take place on Sunday mornings, and sometimes during the week or on Saturday evenings as well.

At the entry to most villages, you find two signs, each with a church symbol and the times of services. The yellow symbol indicates the Roman Catholic services, the mauve symbol the Protestant services.

There are about 40,000 Jews living in Germany, organised in the Central Council of Jews in Germany. The largest Jewish communities are in Berlin and in Frankfurt am Main. There are also at least 1.7 million Muslims living in Germany, most of them Turkish nationals.

Addresses of religious communities
Protestant: Kirchenamt der Evangelischen Kirche in Deutschland, Herrenhäuser Str. 12, D-30419 Hannover, Germany.
Catholic: Sekretariat der Deutschen Bischofskonferenz, Kaiserstr. 163, D-53113 Bonn, Germany.
Jewish: Zentralrat der Juden in Deutschland, Rüngsdorfer Str. 6, D-53173 Bonn, Germany.

CASE STUDIES

Claire the secretary
'My working day as a bilingual secretary/PA in London was becoming routine. I wanted a new challenge, and there was no room for development within the company I was working for. I always wanted to go abroad, and I decided to do it while I was still young and independent,

and before my daughter reached school age. I decided to go to Germany, because I speak and write the language fluently, and because it seemed a safe country, a place where I could take my child without fearing for her safety and health.'

Sarah the student

'I had arranged to spend a year, between A levels and university, in Australia with the GAP project. Everything was signed and sorted, but fell through at the last minute. I was upset and at a loss what I was going to do with my year off. I had been given deferred entrance at Birmingham University. I decided to go to Germany as an au pair.'

Kevin the builder

'I'm a qualified bricklayer, and I was out of work for over a year. Not much hope of finding something new at my age either. I'm 54. When I heard that Germany needed experienced workers for building sites, I made up my mind.'

2
Looking at the Economy

Germany is one of the leading industrial countries. In terms of world trade, Germany holds the second place in the world, and with regard to overall economic performance, Germany comes third.

The country rose from the devastation of the Second World War to its present position among the major industrial nations, with little finance and limited natural resources. The crucial factor which made this so-called *Wirtschaftswunder* (economic miracle) possible was a highly skilled and motivated workforce.

Germany has a social market economy. The Grundgesetz (basic law) guarantees private property and enterprise, and consumers decide freely how to spend their money. The state does not intervene directly in price and wage fixing, but uses subventions and grants to stimulate or support certain industries or social groups. The theme is 'As little government as possible, as much government as necessary'.

COMPARING EAST AND WEST

Western Germany
Before unification, West Germany had a large current account surplus, and national debt was moderate. Its advantages over competing countries were the highly skilled and motivated workforce, high technical standards, high productivity, successful scientists, extensive and reliable infrastructure, a stable Deutschmark, a steady political situation and social harmony.

However, production in Germany was expensive: there were the high wages and social security contributions, company taxes and contributions for safeguarding the environment. These costs, added up and distributed per work hour, are more than in any other country.

Eastern Germany
Developing the eastern German economy will remain a challenge for

several years. Under the socialist regime, the economy was centrally planned, which made it almost impossible for the people to show entrepreneurial spirit, to act on their own responsibility. Now the entire national economy has to change to fit into the West German principles of a social market economy.

Major problems are environmental damage which is costly to repair, infrastructure which is not up to western standards, low productivity (in 1970 it was less than 50 per cent of West Germany's), and, after unification, high unemployment.

During the first phase of the united Germany, the citizens in the east were keen to buy the high quality western products, and western businesses were keen to export their goods there. Western supermarkets opened branches in the east, staffed with western personnel and stocked with western goods.

As a result, eastern shops, factories and businesses folded up. Many East Germans lost their jobs and their spending power. Some sectors of the economy showed a rapid downwards movement. To make matters worse, some of East Germany's traditional export markets had collapsed as well.

Western companies soon realised that if they wanted to sell to the east, they had to give the East Germans the jobs and the income so they could buy products. It took a little longer for them to understand that they also had to buy and use eastern goods in the west if they wanted to improve the economy.

The next development was that some western companies transferred part of their production to eastern Germany, where staff were skilled but production costs were still lower.

The German government made improving the infrastructure a priority. Over 100 billion Deutschmark from public funds have gone into developing eastern Germany. The organisation which has played the key role in the developing and restructuring is the Treuhandanstalt (Trust Agency). It oversees the privatisation and reorganisation of companies and helps them to become competitive.

GERMANY'S TOP TWELVE

The largest companies in Germany are:

1. Stuttgart-based Daimler-Benz AG in the automotive, engineering, aerospace and electrical sector, with 375,000 staff and an annual turnover of DM 98,550 million.

2. Wolfsburg-based car manufacturer Volkswagen AG, with 273,000 staff and an annual turnover of DM 84,400 million.

3. Electrical and engineering company Siemens AG in München, with a workforce of 410,000 and a turnover of DM 78,400 million.

4. Veba AG in Düsseldorf in the energy and chemicals sector, with 129,800 staff and DM 66,400 million turnover.

5. Bundespost Telekom in Bonn in the field of telecommunications, with 232,000 staff and DM 52,500 million turnover.

6. RWE AG, based in Essen, in the energy and building sector, which has 113,600 staff and a turnover of DM 52,400 million.

7. Hoechst AG in Frankfurt which produces chemicals and pharmaceuticals, and has a workforce of 117,700 and an annual turnover of DM 45,500 million.

8. Ludwigshafen-based BASF AG, in the chemical and energy sector, with 123,300 staff and DM 44,500 million turnover.

9. Bayer AG in Leverkusen, which produces chemicals and pharmaceuticals, employs 156,400 staff and achieves a turnover of DM 41,200 million.

10. Thyssen AG in Duisburg in the steel and machinery sector, with a workforce of 147,300 and a turnover of DM 35,800 million.

11. Bosch GmbH in Stuttgart which makes electrical and engineering products, employs 147,300 people and has a turnover of DM 34,400 million.

12. Bayerische Motorenwerke in München, known as a car manufacturer under the initials BMW, which has 73,600 staff and a turnover of DM 31,200 million.

SECTORS OF THE ECONOMY

Vehicle manufacture
This branch of German industry is strong in the east as well as in the west, and accounts for 14.6 per cent of the total industry turnover.

Germany is the third largest automotive producer in the world (after Japan and the USA). About 3,000 companies employ some 750,000 workers and achieve an annual turnover of DM 233 billion. Between four and five million vehicles are manufactured every year, half of them for export.

Thüringen, Sachsen, Niedersachsen, Hessen, Bayern, Saarland and Baden-Württemberg have major vehicle manufacture companies.

Mechanical engineering

There are around 7,000 companies involved in mechanical engineering, most of them in the western part of Germany. The majority of these businesses are small. Only 3 per cent have 1,000 or more staff. In fact, the majority employ fewer than 300 people. The range of mechanical engineering products in Germany is wider than in most other countries: an estimated 17,000 different products, from printing and agricultural machinery to consoles and machine tools. The annual turnover of this sector is DM 222 billion, and the workforce consists of almost 1.2 million people. Around 40 per cent of the goods are exported. One centre of mechanical engineering is Sachsen.

Chemical industry

In this sector, Germany is among the world leaders. About half of the products are exported. In particular, the three giants Bayer, BASF and Hoechst have a reputation for state-of-the-art technology. There are also many successful medium-sized companies. The demand for protection of the environment has put this industry under pressure; as a result, the German chemical industry is pioneering new approaches in some areas. East Germany has had its own strong chemical industry, but it could not compete with the giants in the west, and had severe difficulties with environmental protection. The total workforce employed in Germany's chemical industry is estimated at 655,000, and the annual turnover at around DM 200 billion. Major chemical industries are based in Brandenburg, Rheinland-Pfalz and Sachsen-Anhalt.

Electrical engineering

This industry achieves an annual turnover of DM 225 billion with 1.1 million employees. In the eastern part of Germany, electrical engineering has suffered because of unification.

Communication technology

While Germany has fallen behind international competition in the fields of microchips, data processing and consumer electronics, communication technology is doing well. Hannover is the seat of important communication technology industries. The major employer in this industry sector is Telekom, a privatised part of the former state-owned Deutsche Bundespost, which supplied postal, telecommunications and banking services.

Food processing
A workforce of 575,000 achieves a turnover of DM 219 billion. Some of the biggest companies are in Berlin, Bremen and Saarland.

Textiles and clothing
This industry sector has around 345,00 employees and produces a turnover of DM 219 million. Important companies are in Berlin.

Steel industry
With a workforce of 180,000, Germany has a turnover of around DM 43 million. Brandenburg, Saarland and Nordrhein-Westfalen have a strong steel industry.

Mining
A turnover of DM 35 billion is achieved by 225,000 people. Mining for coal, lignite, silver and other raw materials takes places mostly in Nordrhein-Westfalen, Rheinland-Pfalz, Brandenburg, Sachsen, Sachsen-Anhalt and Niedersachsen.

Precision engineering and optical industry
Small and medium-sized companies, employing about 145,000 staff, dominate this industry. Turnover is around DM 20 billion a year, and production is largely export-orientated. Major industries are in Hessen, Baden-Württemberg and Thüringen.

Environmental protection technology
German companies are the pioneers in this field and have the largest share (more than 20 per cent) of international trade.

Crafts and trades
Although the number of small craft businesses has declined from 900,000 in 1949 to 650,000 in 1993, the number of people working in this area has increased. Each small craft business employs on average eight people. This sector plays an important part in developing the

eastern German economy, because even in the days of central planning many small firms had been able to exist alongside the state-owned units.

In Germany, only a master craftsperson or someone holding an equivalent qualification may carry out a trade, so the services supplied are of a high standard.

Agriculture

The number of farms has decreased from 1.6 million farms which provided work and income for 3.9 million people in 1950, to 580,000 farms with fewer than 540,000 people working there in 1992.

At the same time, productivity increased. In 1950, the average farm worker produced food for ten people, today for over seventy. In western Germany, small and medium-size holdings with less than 50 hectares (120 acres) dominate. Farms produce milk, pork, beef, cereals and sugarbeet. In some regions, wine plays a role (Rheinland-Pfalz, Hessen, Baden-Württemberg), in others, fruit (Hessen, Baden-Württemberg) and vegetables.

In eastern Germany, production co-operatives with mass production of fruit, cereals, vegetables or livestock dominated the agricultural sector. The government has privatised them now and encourages family farm units.

Forestry

About one-third of Germany's surface is covered by forest, including some well-known areas such as the Schwarzwald (Black Forest). Rheinland-Pfalz is the state with the highest proportion of woods; in the eastern part of Germany, Thüringen has extensive forestry.

Between 30 and 40 million cubic metres of timber is felled annually. The main problems are air pollution and acid rain which are depleting the German forests despite protective measures.

Fishery

Over-fishing with modern catching methods affects Germany like other countries. In 1992, the fishing industry employed 48,000 people and had a turnover of DM 11.3 billion. It is particularly strong in Mecklenburg-Westpommern.

Wholesale and retail

The wholesale trade's turnover in 1992 was estimated at about one trillion DM. Around 20,000 wholesalers are registered with the chambers of commerce in eastern Germany, and about 126,000 in western Germany.

There are 400,000 retailers in western Germany who employ 2.5 million staff. In the eastern part of Germany, 550,000 people work in retail.

Energy

Despite successful measures to reduce energy consumption, Germany is one of the world's largest energy consumers. Since unification, lignite has been the main domestic source of energy. Lignite is mined in Rheinland-Pfalz, Brandenburg, Sachsen, Sachsen-Anhalt and Niedersachsen.

Pitcoal is mined in the Ruhr region in Nordrhein-Westfalen and Saarland. It used to account for three-quarters of Germany's energy consumption, but has now dropped to below 18 per cent.

Oil, mostly imported, contributes 41.5 per cent of the energy supplies. Gas is found locally, especially in the North Sea and the Emsland region, as well as imported. Around 18 per cent of the energy consumed is gas.

Germany does not produce uranium, but imports it for the nuclear power stations. About one-third of Germany's electricity is generated by nuclear power.

Banking and finance

Germany's central national bank is the Bundesbank, based in Frankfurt am Main. Its main task is safeguarding the currency, which is one of the most stable currencies in the world. The Bundesbank has responsibility for the country's economic stability. Only the Bundesbank has the power to issue banknotes, and it handles the national currency reserves.

There are 3,392 credit co-operatives, 734 savings banks, 567 foreign banks, 342 lending banks, 35 mortgage banks, 34 building societies and twelve giro clearing banks in Germany, each with their own branch networks.

The financial sector – including savings, loans, stocks and shares – has grown significantly. The German banks' assets rose from DM3 trillion in 1988 to over DM 4 trillion in 1992. Germany's stock exchanges achieved a record turnover of DM 4.6 trillion in 1992. This was 1.2 trillion more than in the previous year.

The exchange in Frankfurt is the largest in Germany, and one of the largest in the world (following New York and Tokyo, and equalling London).

Transport

The transport networks in eastern Germany need modernising and updating, and receive large subsidies which will run into several billions of DM by the year 2000. The transport links between east and west receive priority.

The two public railway systems, the Deutsche Bundesbahn (DB, of West Germany) and the Deutsche Reichsbahn (RB, of East Germany) are being privatised.

In 1992, there were 45 million registered vehicles, most of them cars. The network of trunk roads is 226,000 km long. This includes 11,000 km of Autobahn (motorways).

Experts predict further growth of the transport sector: 30 per cent growth in road passenger transport, 40 per cent in rail passenger transport, 100 per cent in air traffic, 95 per cent in road freight traffic, 55 per cent in rail freight traffic and waterway traffic.

Tourism and catering

Nearly half of all Germans spend their holidays in their own country. Only 12 per cent of overnight stays are by foreign nationals, who spend about DM 17 billion a year.

From May to October 1994, hotels registered 182 million overnight stays. There was a slight decline against the previous year in the west, and a steep increase in the east of Germany, especially in East Berlin.

The sea climate, coasts and islands of the North Sea attract many tourists. The Central Uplands, the Alps and the lakeland areas in Mecklenburg and Holstein are popular with hikers, and Bodensee (Lake Constance) and the lakes in Bavaria are good for water sports.

Romantic landscapes are found in the river valleys, especially along the rivers Rhein (Rhine), Main, Mosel (Moselle), Donau (Danube), Neckar and Elbe.

Germany promotes just under 100 special tourist routes which are away from the main traffic. The German Wine Route and the Romantic Route (which leads through picturesque medieval towns) are the best known.

The hotel and catering trade in Germany shows great seasonal fluctuation in areas where it depends largely on tourism. May to September is the major tourist season, although events like the Bavarian Christmas markets, the Carnival along the river Rhein in February, the wine festivals in autumn and the winter skiing areas in Bavaria also attract visitors.

Publishing

Large publishing houses, including Springer, Süddeutscher Verlag, Verlag DuMont Schauberg, FAZ Gruppe, Bauer Verlag and Burda, dominate the German publishing scene.

According to the Statistisches Bundesamt (Federal Statistical Office), there were 2,716 publishing houses in Germany in 1992, which published 1,477 newspapers and 9,010 magazines.

At the end of 1992, publishers employed 290,800 people, including 22,700 senior journalists and sub-editors. This figure does not include freelances.

The turnover of the publishing industry was DM 41.9 milliards, of which DM 18.8 mrd came from distribution and DM 19.2 mrd from advertising.

In terms of newspapers per 1,000 inhabitants, Germany comes fourth worldwide, behind Japan, the UK and Switzerland. On workdays about 410 newspapers appear in Germany. They publish almost 1,650 local and regional editions, and the total circulation is about 31.3 million. Over two-thirds of all newspapers are bought by subscription, the rest are sold at newsagents, in shops and on the streets. The best-selling subscription paper is the *Westdeutsche Allgemeine Zeitung*, and the leading tabloid (and *Sun* equivalent) is *Bildzeitung*.

More than 8,000 magazines are published in Germany, including *Der Spiegel*, *Stern* and *Bunte*. For examples of German magazines, see pages 115-119.

Foreign trade

In 1992, Germany imported goods to the value of DM 637.8 billion, and exported DM 670.6 billion. Nearly every third employed person in Germany works direct for export. The most important imported goods are agricultural products such as foodstuffs, electrical goods, and textiles. Among the major export products are industrial equipment, machinery, motor vehicles, chemical products, and electrical engineering products.

The development of the European market has meant that intra-European trade increased. In 1992, more than half of Germany's exports went to European Community member states. Germany's main trading partner is France.

The major purchaser of German goods is France, followed by Italy, the UK, the Netherlands, Belgium/Luxembourg, and the USA.

Germany imports most goods from France, followed by the Netherlands, Italy, Belgium/Luxembourg, the UK and the USA.

USEFUL ADDRESSES

Bundesverband der Deutschen Industrie (Federation of German Industries), Gustav-Heinemann-Ufer 84–88, D-50968 Köln, Germany.

Zentralverband des Deutschen Handwerks (Federation of German Crafts and Trades), Johanniterstr. 1, D-53113 Bonn, Germany.

Deutscher Bauernverband (German Farmers' Association), Godesberger Allee 142–148, D-53175 Bonn, Germany.

Hauptverband des Deutschen Einzelhandels (German Retailers' Association), Sachsenring 89, D-50677 Köln, Germany.

Bundesverband des Deutschen Groß- und Außenhandels (Federation of German Wholesale and Foreign Trade), Kaiser-Friedrich-Str. 13, D-53113 Bonn, Germany.

Bundesverband Deutscher Banken (Federation of Commercial Banks), Mohrenstr. 35–51, D-50670 Köln, Germany.

Deutscher Sparkassen- und Giroverband (German Association of Public Savings and Girobanks), Simrockstr. 4, D-53113 Bonn, Germany.

Bundesverband der Deutschen Volksbanken und Raiffeisenbanken e.V. (Federation of German Co-operative Banks), Heussallee 5, D-53113 Bonn, Germany.

Ausstellungs- und Messeausschuß der Deutschen Wirtschaft (German Council of Trade Fairs and Exhibitions), Lindenstr. 8, D-50674 Köln, Germany.

Deutsche Zentrale für Tourismus (German National Tourist Board), Beethovenstr. 69, D-60325 Frankfurt, Germany.

Deutscher Fremdenverkehrsverband e.V. (Tourist Industry Association), Niebuhrstr. 16b, D-53123 Bonn, Germany.

Bundesverband Deutscher Zeitungsverleger (Federation of German Newspaper Publishers), Riemenschneiderstr. 10, D-53175 Bonn, Germany.

Deutscher Journalistenverband (German Journalists Association) Bennauerstr. 60, D-63115 Bonn, Germany.

Verband Deutscher Zeitschriftenverleger (Association of German Periodical Publishers), Winterstr. 50, D-53177 Bonn, Germany.

3
Understanding the Germans

BUILDING LINKS WITH GERMANY

The more you know about Germany, the easier it will be to settle in. There is a lot you can do to absorb German culture and mentality while you are still in your home country, especially if you don't plan to go immediately:

- Find a pen-friend in Germany.
- Get involved in town twinning activities.
- Take in German students for the summer.
- Spend your next holidays in Germany.
- Brush up your German (see Chapter 4).
- Subscribe to German newspapers and magazines (see page 115).
- Join the Anglo-German Association (if you live in the UK).
- Contact the nearest Goethe-Institut.
- Read books about Germany.

THE ANGLO-GERMAN ASSOCIATION

This is a registered charity which promotes friendship and understanding between Germany and the UK. It organises events in the London area, and, through affiliated societies, in other areas. It also publishes a newsletter, *Anglo-German Review*. Membership costs £10 a year (£16 for couples).

Address: The Anglo-German Association, 158 Buckingham Palace Road, London SW1W 9TR, UK. Tel: (0171) 259 9922.

THE ANGLO-GERMAN CLUB

This is a club for young people of British and German nationality who meet to share their interest in music, art, films, dance, theatre, food and drink, using both languages. Membership costs £7.50 a year.

Address: Anglo-German Club, PO Box 427, London W8 5QU.

THE GOETHE-INSTITUT

Named after the great German writer, Johann Wolfgang von Goethe, the Goethe-Institut is an organisation dedicated to promoting the German language abroad and to aiding international co-operation in cultural matters.

It has sixteen branches in Germany and 153 branches in 76 countries. Most Goethe-Institut branches organise exhibitions and cultural events in the fields of science, literature, music, films, theatre, newspapers, magazines, and audiovisual materials. They are involved in education, especially in methodology, geography and literature, and organise German language courses and exams.

Address (central administration): Goethe-Institut, Helene-Weber-Allee 1, Postfach 190419, D-80604 München, Germany. Tel: (089) 159210.

EXPLORING GERMANY IN YOUR HOLIDAYS

If your plans for living and working in Germany are long term rather than immediate, it is useful to spend your next holidays in Germany. It is *not* a good idea to take a coach trip to the Bavarian castles, book a river cruise, or join an activity where you will be mostly in the company of other tourists.

Spend your holidays in one place and get to know the town or village and its people, rather than wasting your time travelling from place to place.

If possible, go on your own. You are more likely this way to make contacts with Germans than if you take friends with you.

Staying with a family

With home-stay holidays, you become part of a German family for a week or more. They are usually cheaper than hotel accommodation, and you get to know the Germans in their daily lives. You share the family's meals and perhaps some of their leisure activities, and they can introduce you to neighbours and friends who share your hobbies or work in the same industry.

Home-stay holidays are useful if you already speak a little German, as some host families don't understand English. If possible, ask the travel agent to arrange for a stay where you are the only paying guest of the family.

Price example: One week with single room, bed and breakfast in Zell (near Frankfurt am Main), including return flight from Heathrow, organised by Moswin Tours, £439. For information on other home-stay holidays in Germany, contact the German National Tourist Office.

Special interest holidays

There are surprisingly few travel organisers who offer holidays which allow the traveller to mix with Germans in Germany. For most special interest and hobby holidays, the tourists stay among themselves.

You can make your own arrangements, perhaps through your club or group which may have an equivalent in Germany, or by booking a language course with work experience (see page 50). You may be able to plan an exchange or visit with the advice of your town twinning officer.

Moswin Tours Ltd organises 'wine holidays', where you live and work with the locals. You spend a week with a wine-grower in the Moseltal (Moselle Valley), one of Germany's major wine-growing regions. You stay at a vintner's house, and help him or her with the day-to-day work at the vineyard. Depending on the time of year, this can range from tending of the vine in the field to wine-making in the cellar. You can talk to the wine farmer and learn firsthand about the wine as a living product in the environment in which it is produced.

One week in a double room with bed and breakfast, and including the return flight from Heathrow, costs £376. These holidays are available from May to September.

During harvest time in October, when the vintners are too busy to teach and explain their work, Moswin Tours Ltd offers a one-week holiday. This includes sightseeing tours and a river cruise as well as two or three days' work alongside local grape harvesters in the vineyards. The organiser explains: 'This tour is for people with a genuine interest in wine making, who do not mind getting their hands dirty in the steep vineyards and in the cellars.'

Addresses

German National Tourist Office, Nightingale House, 65 Curzon Street, London W1Y 7PE, UK. Tel: (0171) 411 3400. Fax: (0171) 411 3400.

Deutsche Zentrale für Tourismus, Beethovenstr. 69, D-60325 Frankfurt, Germany. Tel: (069) 75720. Fax: (069) 751903.

Moswin Tours Ltd, Moswin House, 21 Church Street, Oadby, Leicester LE2 5DB. Tel: (0116) 271992. Fax: (0116) 2716016.

DIFFERENT ATTITUDES

Like all nationalities, the Germans have typical characteristics and behave in ways which are natural to the natives, but may seem odd to other nationals.

Which of these you experience, and to which extent, depends of course on the German society in which you move. Students differ in their attitudes from OAPs, city dwellers from village folk. Every German is different, and it would be foolish to expect 80 million individuals to think and act all in the same way.

Regard the following as attitudes you are likely to meet when in Germany, but don't assume that every German turns out to be exactly like this.

Being a foreigner

As a British, Irish, New Zealand, Australian, Canadian or US national, Germans will regard you as superior to 'other foreigners', probably because of shared ethnic roots, similar appearance, similar political and religious beliefs, economic systems and wealth. The same applies to Scandinavians, Swiss, Austrians and French people.

Most Germans like meeting foreigners and exchanging ideas and views. However, many Germans are concerned that too many foreign nationals are living in Germany – currently 6.5 million. Racists and nationalists are a minority and don't represent the German government or the German people as a whole. However, this minority group is active and can make life unpleasant for foreigners. You are not likely to become a victim of their activities if you are western, northern or central European. But you may encounter prejudice and sometimes hostility if you are Southern or Eastern European, Black African, Asian, Arab, Turkish or South American.

If your neighbours or colleagues are hesitant about making friends with you, or if you feel that they are watching you carefully, especially in rural areas, give them time. However, if you face repeated active hostilities from several people, it shows that the particular neighbourhood has a strong racist attitude. Simply move to another town quarter or area.

Why everyone is 'English'

Don't be surprised if Germans have never heard of the United Kingdom of Great Britain and Northern Ireland. The phrase is simply too long for Germans to pronounce. Therefore, they'll call it all England.

Germans will be surprised if you, as non-English Britons, object. They may simply not know of your existence.

The average German has heard of Scotland (and knows that it is part of England), but not of Wales. He or she may even think of Ireland as English.

They don't mean an offence. You may want to carry a map of Great Britain, with clearly defined borders, in your pocket.

Clichés

Do you expect the Germans to walk around in Lederhosen and Dirndl, a sausage in one hand and a tankard of beer in the other, dancing the Schuhplattler all the time?

Then you had better know what they expect you to be like: Germans imagine 'Englishmen' (that is, male Britons) to be tall and thin, wearing bowler hats, carrying a black umbrella and reading *The Times*. They know that English women drink tea all the time, stand in the daily rain to greet each other with 'Nice weather, isn't it?' in a high voice. English women wear pearl necklaces and old-fashioned hats in bright pink, an image probably modelled on the Queen, the Queen Mother and Barbara Cartland all rolled into one.

The Germans believe that the English are poor lovers. Why else would they take hot-water bottles to bed?

Of Scotsmen, Germans know that they wear checked skirts and play the bagpipes (Dudelsack); what Scottish women wear or do, they don't even guess.

About the Irish they know little – if they are not English, surely they are at least similar.

Americans are regarded as easy going and superficial. They spend their days on psychiatric couches or riding rodeos, or in their office doing efficient business with their feet on the desk. If they live in New York or Chicago, they spend their time either chasing criminals or being chased by the police, and they all carry revolvers and have their mouths full of chewing gum.

Sense of humour

Many people claim that Germans don't have any sense of humour. The truth is that they have – but they laugh about different jokes. The British custom of calling your dearest friend a 'bloody bastard' and insulting him in public would not work in Germany. A German would be shocked to hear such a conversation, and deeply offended if called by an insulting name. Never would he or she believe that you meant it as a friendly teasing.

There are great regional differences. North Germans laugh about different things from the south Germans, east Germans find other things funny than their western counterparts. What do you think of the following joke:

A driver stops his car at a red traffic light and thinks seriously about life, the universe and everything. He does not notice that the traffic lights have switched to green. A pedestrian knocks on the car window and says: 'Hey, mate, it won't get any greener.'

You wonder where the joke is? So would most Germans. But a true Berliner will assure you the story has a deep and meaningful humour.

If Germans tell jokes, they are usually about other Germans: The Bayern (Bavarians) have jokes about the Preussen (Prussians), the Badener about the Schwaben, and all Germans except the Ostfriesen (East Frisians) tell Ostfriesen jokes. Since unification, there are also Ossi jokes about eastern Germans. German jokes about other Germans are mild and usually infer that other German tribes are not quite as intelligent as the tribe to which the narrator belongs.

As a foreigner, you can laugh about these jokes (if you find them funny), but don't repeat them elsewhere.

Jokes about miserly Scottish people are also regarded as socially acceptable, although nobody can explain why the Germans should have picked Scots as a target for their fun.

Beware of racist jokes, which are often cruel. Many of them are about Turks and Slavs, and are variations on the jokes told during the Third Reich about Jews. People who spread these jokes are likely to be racists and may belong to nationalist groups. Don't gratify them by laughing at their jokes, but don't make yourself a target for them by protesting, either. Just pretend that you don't understand – after all, you don't speak German well enough, do you?

Germans among themselves

Germany was not always a united nation. For most of its history, it was split into many small states and kingdoms, often at war against each other.

For centuries, the Bayern (Bavarians) and the Preussen (Prussians) were arch-enemies, and they cannot shake off inherited prejudices. A

Bayer and a Preusse can be closest friends, but whenever there is an assembly of either Bayern or Preussen, especially during traditional festivals, they will talk contemptuously of the others.

A similar enmity exists between the inhabitants of Baden (the Badener) and of Württemberg (the Schwaben). Since their states were united in Baden-Württemberg they have been competing with each other, each blaming the other for the bad things in the state, such as pollution or traffic jams. A single Schwabe in a group of Badener may be subject to a lot of jokes and teasing. Nowadays, this 'enmity' is just a game which is heartily reciprocated by the other party.

Don't take it seriously if members of German states insult each other – the Germans don't either.

Don't take part in the game, as the rules are complex. A German friend who patiently explains to you the rules of the game is likely to make fun of both you and the 'enemies' by setting you up.

Take care you pronounce the names of the ethnic groups correctly. A person from Baden is a Badener. Only a Schwabe has the right to call him or her a 'Badenser', and the Badener has the right to take this as an insult. While the Badener will regard this insult as acceptable from a Schwabe, he or she will not accept it from a foreigner, and at the worst it may cost you a friendship or a job.

A Schwabe may call him- or herself a 'Schwob', but if a Badener uses the same word, the Schwabe may be offended.

You can see that this matter is delicate and complicated. Stick to the official High German names of the peoples, and you cannot go far wrong.

Beach towels and all that
Germans won't believe they have a world-wide reputation for placing their towels around swimming pools and on deck-chairs.

Half the Germans will respond to this information with: 'Oh, but I would never do that, why should I?'

The other half say, wondering: 'But how else can I keep the deck-chair vacant while I'm away?'

Women
In Germany, it is important for men to show that they are not chauvinists. Making friends with radical feminists and talking about equality at every opportunity helps. However, most Germans pay only lip-service to equality. Traditionally, women had to dedicate themselves to the three Ks: Kinder, Küche, Kirche (children, kitchen, church).

Most women leave the three Ks behind them and follow a career or other interests, but they do so guiltily. Only a few women are represented in the top positions in industry, or in the Bundestag. The situation is improving, but slowly.

Measures taken to aid equality are seldom of practical use for women – shop opening hours are still inconvenient for the working mother, for example – but a matter of displaying political correctness. For example, after many years of male heads on Germany's postage stamps, a series with women was launched. Unfortunately, these show only the denomination, the head and the name. Even the Germans don't know who the depicted women are and what they have achieved.

Class system

In Germany, it is not as important as in the UK into which class you were born or at which school you were educated. Most pupils, however wealthy, attend a state school. There is even a stigma attached to private boarding-schools. Many Germans think 'These poor children, deserted by their parents'.

It is almost impossible to judge from the language someone uses whether they belong to the working, middle or upper classes.

Clothing

Germans are intolerant about clothing. Everything other than 'normal' dress is frowned upon. Only the daring walk down the streets in an outfit they expect to be all the rage next year.

People will stare at you if you wear a saree or a kilt, point their fingers at you, and whisper behind your back.

Model your own clothing style on that of your friends, neighbours and colleagues. If you want to make a statement by your choice of clothing, perhaps by wearing unbleached cotton or T-shirts with political slogans, you'd better choose the statements the other people around you make.

In rural areas, you are expected to wear your Sunday best on the day of the Lord.

Don't mention the war

Many Germans are pacifists, and an even greater number are sympathetic to the pacifist cause. If there is a war somewhere in the world, most Germans feel grief. Even if they agree that great wrong has been done, they suggest the need to continue with trade embargoes and negotiation when most other countries have already prepared their military involvement.

During the Iran/Kuwait war, when the British were enthusiastic about sending soldiers, the Germans marched in silence, carrying peace banners. Your German friends will be shocked if you call for a military solution to a political problem.

This German attitude dates from the first years after World War II. The Germans, who had suffered even more than other peoples from the war, declared that never again should a war originate from German soil. Therefore, young Germans were brought up to value peace higher than military achievements.

You can talk about World Wars I and II, as long as you treat the wars as a devastating illness from which both your nations suffered and which is now overcome. If you start glorifying the war and your and your ancestors' role in it, you will quickly find yourself in a Cold War with your German friends.

However, the Germans are quite happy discussing politics in a pub, and they can do it without being at each other's throats.

Toys

Never give military toys – fighter aircraft, tanks, machine guns – as gifts to children. Germans are great believers in 'Abrüstung im Kinderzimmer' (disarmament in the nursery). They reason that children should not learn to regard war as a game, and killing as a pastime. A toyshop selling war toys at Christmas time would be boycotted by all its customers.

There is no clear definition of 'war toys'. As a rough guidance, anything used for war purposes in the western world in the twentieth century is taboo. Ethnic weapons (such as African spears or Indian tomahawks), and historic weapons (swords, cannons, tin soldiers) are acceptable.

Green, greener, greenest

The Germans take the environment seriously. You may get a *Moralpredigt* (moral sermon) if your friends discover that you use non-recycled loo paper or washing-powder with phosphates. It is important not only to be a green, but to prove it. Ask your friends for advice – they will be happy to train you in how to scrub the sink with ecologically sound vinegar. For more information about the subject, see pages 135-139.

Environmental matters are an acceptable conversation topic even during a first meeting or a romantic date. The number one subject is the *Waldsterben*, the dying of forests because of air pollution.

Animals

The animal rights movement in Germany is not as strong as in the UK. Free-range eggs and vegetarian food are available, but not much in demand. You can see fur coats worn in the streets and displayed in shop-windows, and nobody splashes them with paint or smashes in windows.

It is all right to discuss the subject with your friends, but it is not acceptable to challenge a fur-clad woman in the street or to be rude.

Many Germans keep a dog, especially a German shepherd or a poodle. Germans identify with their dogs who are just how they see themselves: strong, intelligent, loyal, alert. Never criticise someone's dog.

Charities

Charities play a less important role in Germany than in the UK, perhaps because the social network is better. Fewer people are involved in fund-raising. The Germans would shake their heads at the thought that they should wear a red plastic nose or do a bungee jump to support a charity: if they want to give money, they will give the money without such fuss. Charity is a serious matter, and it would not be proper to act silly.

However, German groups and clubs compete for a mention in the *Guiness Book of Records* by baking the biggest bread loaf or the longest sausage. The press and television are present when slices of bread or sausage are sold, and the proceeds go to a children's charity.

Healthy eating

Germans are concerned about what they eat. For months after the Chernobyl catastrophe, they did not eat strawberries or mushrooms or drink milk, because they were radioactive. Citizens' initiative groups handed out warning leaflets, although official government statements said the food was safe. They could not believe that the British, whose crops were almost equally affected, did not care at all.

There are few vegetarians in Germany. Restaurateurs and chefs take it as a personal insult if you ask for a dish without meat. They will tell you positively that their meat is tender, hygienic and fresh. Even if you persuade them to bring you a salad because you don't eat meat, it may contain bacon. Some progressive restaurants have a vegetarian section in their menu, which contains such specialities as asparagus with ham.

Knitting

German women are supposed to spend their days knitting, just as in the middle ages they were expected to spin. Surprisingly, they enjoy it. If you have a German boyfriend, it is good practice to knit him a jumper or two.

Knitting (*stricken*) is socially acceptable in almost every situation as long as the hands are not needed for other purposes. You can see Germans busily knitting in commuter trains, while watching TV, during lessons at schools, college and university (few teachers will object), and even in the Bundestag.

Knitting is no longer limited to women. Young men do it, too. What better way of putting those boring hours at college to good use?

Personal hygiene

Most Germans prefer having a shower to having a bath. And with living space at a premium, many modern flats are equipped with a shower cubicle but no bath-tub.

German women do not shave their legs or underarms, unless their limbs are covered in particularly dark and thick hair. Shaving is considered 'unnatural', and not necessary for hygienic purposes. If you are used to seeing smooth legs in your home country, you may find hairy German legs unattractive. On the other hand, some German men find shaved female skin unpleasant. It reminds them of plucked chicken.

Over the last few years, the cosmetics and electrical appliances industry in Germany has worked hard at persuading German women that body hair is unattractive. More and more Germans use wax, gels and shavers. Today you can shave or not, and won't offend either way.

Ordnungsliebe

This means 'love of regulations and order'. *Ordnung* includes everything: from lawfulness to tidiness, from honesty to proper behaviour. There are many proverbs and sayings which include the word *Ordnung*. You will hear the Germans say '*Ordnung muß sein*' (everything must be ordered) and '*Alles in Ordnung*' (literally: everything according to law and order; meaning: everything's fine). The Germans are proud of their efficiency, punctuality and discipline, and expect foreigners to admire these attributes.

Angst

The German word *Angst* has been taken up by several languages. The Germans would be horrified to know this. *Angst* means fear, anxiety, and the Germans wouldn't want the world to regard cowardice as a national characteristic.

The Germans are not afraid of many matters. But they are concerned, anxious, and worried more seriously than other people about the environment, about their health, about the threat of a nuclear war and about war in general. Of course, they also worry about anything which would endanger law and order, about failure (which is why they check each and everything a dozen times), about radioactivity, and about being without money. Fairly new in the list of major anxieties are unemployment and, depending on political viewpoint, either foreigners or racism.

In their book *Xenophobe's Guide to the Germans*, Stefan Zeidenitz and Ben Barkow explain how the Germans justify their *Angst:* 'Secretly, they believe it takes a superior intelligence to realise just how dangerous life really is. They see their anxiety as proportional to their intellectual capabilities.'

Queueing

Germans form queues at supermarket tills and in the works canteen, but not at bus-stops.

CASE STUDIES

Claire

'I know Germany from my school days, when I was on an exchange visit. What came as a surprise was that deep concern about peace and the environment. The Germans take these subjects seriously.'

Sarah

'I didn't have a clue about Germany before I went. I had heard the Germans were arrogant and unfriendly. There are some arrogant Germans, I grant you, but fewer than arrogant Britons in the UK. Just because Germans get their towel on a sunbed first doesn't mean they are an arrogant nation.

'If a German gets to the sunbed before an English person, they are considered arrogant. But if an English person gets there before a German, the German won't even think about it. They just choose another sunbed, that's it. So who has the problem?

'Okay, there is a difference between Germans and the English, and I think the problem is that Germans are not afraid to say what they mean. The English are more likely to talk around a subject, and may be offended when the Germans just come out with a comment. A question that would take an English gentleman four hours to ask would take a German half a minute.'

Kevin

'It all happened so quickly that I had little time to find out more about Germany. I arrived with many prejudices. I imagined the Germans would all be tall and blond, military-minded, wearing Lederhosen, eating black bread and drinking beer. I think my image of the Germans was a bit like a cartoon character. Mind you, they *do* drink a lot of beer.'

CHECKLIST

1. How much do I know about Germany?

2. Have I ever been there?

3. Do I know any Germans?

4. What can I do to meet Germans?

5. How can I find out more about Germany?

6. What books, magazines, newspapers could I get hold of?

7. What about spending a holiday in Germany? Where would I stay?

4
Learning the Language

Your chances of finding a job, and of settling in happily, depend heavily on your knowledge of the language. The better your German, the easier everything becomes. So if you are considering going to live in Germany, start learning or brushing up your German *now*.

STUDYING GERMAN BEFORE YOU GO

Most adult education centres run classes at beginners, intermediate and advanced levels, as well as conversation classes and sometimes even courses in German for business or for tourism.

The Goethe-Institut has branches in Dublin, Glasgow, York, Manchester and London, as well as in other cities worldwide. Their German courses are structured and standardised so you can take one or more units in your home country and continue when you are in Germany.

You can also buy a home study course (for example, from Linguaphone), and if money is tight, you can borrow one from your local library.

Another low-cost way of brushing up your German is subscribing to a German magazine or newspaper. You learn modern phrases, as well as the vocabulary of your hobby or profession. See page 115.

STUDYING GERMAN IN GERMANY

The best way to learn not only the language, but also about the country and the people, is in the country itself. If you can afford it, spend a holiday in Germany and combine it with a language course.

There are courses at all levels, and what you learn in the morning you can put to use in the afternoon.

How do you make the most of your language course? Madeleine Kötter of the DID (Deutsch in Deutschland) language school advises:

'Naturally, participants must be motivated to achieve the highest possible learning result. But where adult students are concerned, this is almost always the case.'

She adds: 'Most of our students come from France, Italy, Switzerland and Spain. Recently, we've had many from Eastern Europe, especially Poland, and there are always some students from Japan and Latin America. We have several students who plan to work in Germany, as well as some who already have a job here and need to study the language intensively. These are often employees of large German companies, or of foreign companies with German subsidiaries.'

At Horizonte in Regensburg, the students are from seventy different countries, mostly from Italy, Spain, Ireland, France and Great Britain. Managing director Martin Mayer suggests: 'To get maximum benefit from a course, you should acquire basic language skills beforehand. For a beginner, this could mean about ten lessons in a standard textbook. This eases the start, and it enables you to communicate from the beginning.'

He says that among the Horizonte students, there are several unemployed graduates from other countries, mostly Italy and Spain, who are looking for work in Germany and study the language to increase their prospects.

At Kapito, a language school in Münster, most students are from Spain, Italy, the Scandinavian countries, France and Great Britain. Hansgerd Schomacher says: 'Students can contribute to the success of the course by preparing and revising the lessons.'

Sonia Waldmann of BWS Germanlingua recommends 'active participation in the course, as well as contacts with German teachers, host families and the native population' for maximum benefit.

GERMAN FOR SPECIAL PURPOSES

Some schools offer specialist classes for professional people, covering the terminology of a particular trade. This is useful for job-hunters as well as for those who already have a job.

At Kapito, Hansgerd Schomacher explains: 'We run language classes especially for the areas of business, tourism, law, medicine and technology. These courses – especially the German for Business course – are popular with staff who know they will be working in Germany. They come from various sectors and professions: sales people, secretaries, managers and so on.'

An intensive two-week course with 60 lessons in groups of three to five students costs £1,650 at Kapito, including lunch. Bed and breakfast can be booked for an extra £300.

Martin Mayer of Horizonte says: 'Most of our students book a course in general German, and they may follow it up with a course in German for business or tourism. We also offer courses for translators.'

BWS Germanlingua is a school which provides courses in business-related German, German for hotel and catering and for tourism, as well as advanced teacher training. Venues are Grün (a small village in the Bavarian Forest), Deggendorf, Regensburg and Passau.

Madeleine Kötter of the DID explains: 'We offer classes in German for tourism, for business, for banking, and for nurses. The greatest demand is for business and economy related courses. Most participants are executives. The Bank of England has sent staff on our courses several times. Our course German for Commerce is often booked by secretaries and economy or business students. German for nurses is becoming increasingly popular.'

In addition, the DID provides trade fair training. Students learn how to talk to customers, how to present products and services and how to conduct small talk, as well as learning about topical matters currently discussed in the industry sectors. This course can be as long or as short as the participants wish.

The DID offers individual one-to-one tuition in Berlin, Frankfurt am Main and München, and sometimes other cities. Tuition in groups is possible only in Frankfurt.

A two-week DID course in German for Business with 35 lessons a week in a small group of four or five people, staying with a German family in a single room with bed, breakfast and dinner, costs DM 3,180. A course in economic German for students and young adults with 29 lessons a week, staying with a German family in a single or double room with bed, breakfast and dinner, costs DM 2,190.

LANGUAGE COURSES WITH WORK EXPERIENCE

Some language schools arrange work experience placements for their students: several weeks of language studies are followed by several weeks in a practical work environment. Work experience with a German firm encourages use of the terminology of the trade, and gives you the confidence you need to succeed in a foreign work environment. It also improves your chances of finding a job if you can mention work experience in Germany in your CV. You can also use your work experience to make contacts in the industry.

However, work experience is only an option if you have the time and money to spend. German firms rarely compensate their work experience people for work done during training.

'We offer work experience in various sectors,' says Madeleine Kötter of DID. 'Most placements are in the commercial and administrative sector, that is within offices, with banks or insurance firms. Work experience in the catering sector, in hotels and restaurants, is also in demand. If required, and if the candidate speaks fluent German and has some work-related skills, we can arrange placements in car manufacturing, in the chemical and pharmaceutical industry, in nursing and so on.'

She says the earlier the participant books the course and the placement, the easier it is to find a placement which is tailor-made for the participant's needs. 'Most people have realistic expectations as far as work experience placements are concerned. However, some overestimate their language skills. Many hope to get a placement for just two or four weeks. This is possible, but the most interesting placements are only available for those who are prepared to stay longer. The companies are not willing to invest in extensive training for someone who is going to leave soon.'

Kapito also arranges work experiences, mostly in the areas of hotels, tourism, foreign trade and manufacturing. 'We visit possible companies in and around Münster and discuss the possibilities of work experience placements. Some of the participants have only a vague idea what they could possibly do during a work experience with a German firm, and how German companies operate.'

He has observed that many students at Kapito learn German with a view to finding employment in Germany – 'especially those who combine a language course with work experience.'

JOINING A UNIVERSITY SUMMER SCHOOL

Regensburg

Some German universities organise summer schools especially for foreign nationals. Subjects vary from university to university and from year to year.

The Universität Regensburg offers three-week courses for undergraduates and graduates. The subject studied during the 1995 course, for example, was '*Einigkeit und Recht und Freiheit*' – Unity, Justice, Peace – Theoretic Ideals and Reality in the German National State in the Nineteenth and Twentieth Centuries'.

Participants must have good German, and only applications in German language will be considered. The course costs £1,000 for bed, breakfast and one additional meal a day, and accommodation is normally in double rooms. Excursions are included in the price.

Trier

Universität Trier is another university which runs summer courses. Participants are allocated to different groups according to their fluency in German. However, there are no beginners' classes. Grammar, vocabulary, conversation, reading and discussing journalistic and literary texts, and pronunciation form the linguist part of a typical course. There are also seminars and lectures on topical issues of German politics, economy, culture, society, language and literature, and guided visits to museums, wine tastings, concerts and films.

The course is suitable for undergraduate and graduate students of any subject, especially of the German language. In 1995, the course ran from 21 August to 16 September. The precise date varies from year to year.

The course fee is currently DM 650, and accommodation costs between DM 320 and DM 380. Students can get cheap meals in the university canteen (between DM 3 and DM 6 for a meal). It is advisable to register early.

Freiburg

The Albert-Ludwigs-Universität in Freiburg offers summer courses at intermediate as well as advanced levels, and students need not necessarily be graduates. Subjects of recent summer courses have included business German as well as contemporary German literature and philosophy. A four-week course costs DM 650 excluding accommodation and meals.

Other possibilities

Other universities and institutions offering summer courses for undergraduate and graduate students are in Augsburg, Bamberg, Bayreuth, Berlin, Bochum, Bonn, Braunschweig, Bremen, Chemnitz, Dresden, Düsseldorf, Eichstätt, Erfurt, Erlangen, Essen, Frankfurt am Main, Fulda, Giessen, Greifswald, Halle, Hannover, Heidelberg, Ilmenau, Jena, Kassel, Kiel, Koblenz, Köthen, Leipzig, Magdeburg, Mainz, Mannheim, Marburg/Lahn, München, Münster, Oldenburg, Osnabrück, Rostock, Saarbrücken, Stuttgart, Tübingen, Weimar, Zwickau. The

Deutscher Akademischer Austauschdienst (DAAD) publishes a brochure of forthcoming courses, dates and venues.

LEARNING AT A GOETHE-INSTITUT

The Goethe-Institut runs standardised German language classes at various levels and venues. Each course lasts eight weeks, with 25 lessons a week, and requires the students to study independently for at least ten extra hours per week. As the courses are standardised, it is possible to do one eight-week unit at one venue, and the next unit in another town, or even in another country.

Venues include Berlin, Iserlohn, Konstanz, Murnau, Rothenburg, Konstanz, Schwäbisch Hall and others. A course costs around DM 2,600, excluding accommodation and meals. The Goethe-Institut also has branches in the UK, the USA, Ireland and other countries.

BOOKING THROUGH CESA

You can book your language holidays direct with the college of your choice and arrange your own transport, or you can use the services of your local travel agent.

The prospect of finding exactly the right course out of a vast range of available courses can be daunting. Travel agents don't always know how to analyse customers' needs for language classes and may be more or less tied to one organiser. You may want to contact an agency which specialises in language courses abroad.

CESA is a language course agent in the UK which liaises with several language schools and colleges in Germany and in other countries. These include Eurocentre in Köln, Colon Fremdspracheninstitut in Hamburg, GLS Sprachenzentrum in Berlin, LGS International House in Freiburg, Lessing-Kolleg in Marburg and DID in München. By liaising with them, CESA is in the best position to recommend a course which meets your needs in terms of length, date, venue, level, contents, intensity, accommodation and budget.

Customers include:

- Business personnel who require language training to help them in a new career or to improve their prospects in a current career.

- Professionals who need to polish their language skills to communicate with foreign clients in a business context.

- Foreign language teachers looking to refresh their linguistic skills or who wish to improve a second language to increase their job prospects.

- University graduates or undergraduates who wish to concentrate on in-depth language training before taking on a new career in law, banking, commerce or management consultancy.

Goethe examinations, private tuition, business German and teacher refresher courses can be arranged.

CASE STUDIES

Claire settles in

'I spoke fluent German before I came to Germany, and this made settling in easy. I don't know how soon I would have found a flat, or a playgroup for my daughter without knowing the language. Some of the German I had learnt at secretarial college turned out to be out of date, especially the phrases for correspondence. But I learnt quickly. I also picked up modern German phrases for everyday life. Perhaps I should have read some contemporary German novels to polish my German before I went.'

Sarah: 'Sink or swim'

'I did not speak a word of German, and now I can speak a lot. I had to either sink or swim. It took me six weeks of sinking and then in the sixth week I started to swim. I had to talk German to the children, and two-year-old Pirmin was the best German teacher I could have.

'My host family also enrolled me for a course, 'German for foreigners', at the adult education centre. I did not gain much from it. The students came from Turkey, Italy, Russia and Siberia, and they were all at different levels of ability. Although I was an absolute beginner, I was just out of college, and so I learnt faster than the others. The teacher tried to help me by giving me extra exercises, but that wasn't enough. Also, the course was all about matters which had no relevance to my daily life, for example how to get permission for fishing in a river. I suppose I could have found another language course at a college, but I learnt enough German from my host family and my friends.'

Kevin struggles with the language

'I still don't speak much German, although I have picked up the phrases needed on the construction site. And I can say, quite fluently, 'A large beer please' and 'Cheers'. I also picked up several swear-words, but I won't mention them here. Sometimes I think life would be easier if I spoke German, but in the evenings I'm just too tired to go to night school.'

USEFUL ADDRESSES

Albert-Ludwigs-Universität Freiburg, Rekorat, Akademisches Auslandsamt, D-79085 Freiburg, Germany. Tel: (0761) 203-0. Fax: (0761) 203-4377.

BWS Germanlingua, Westliche Zwingergasse 11, D-94489 Deggendorf, Germany. Tel: (0991) 37021-0. Fax: (0991) 6812.

CESA Languages Abroad, Western House, Malpas, Truro, TR1 1SQ. Tel: (01872) 225300. Fax: (01872) 225400.

DID Deutsch Institut, Hauptverwaltung, Hauptstr. 26, D-63811 Stockstadt, Germany. Tel: (06027) 447710. Fax: (06027) 417741.

Goethe-Institut, Zentrale Einschreibung, Helene-Weber-Allee 1, D-80604 München, Germany. Tel: (089) 15921-200/206. Fax: (089) 15921-200/202.

Horizonte, Institut für Sprache, Kommunikation und Kultur e.V., Rote Hahnengasse 12, D-93047 Regensburg, Germany. Tel: (09410) 57207. Fax: (09410) 562862.

Kapito, Salzstr. 21, Postfach 8672, D-48046 Münster, Germany. Tel: (0251) 511174. Fax: (0251) 46144.

Universität Regensburg, Lehrgebiet Deutsch als Fremdsprache, Universitätsstr. 31, D-93053 Regensburg, Germany. Tel: (0941) 9432425 (mornings only). Fax: (0941) 9432410.

Universität Trier, Akademisches Auslandsamt, Universitätsring 15, D-54286 Trier, Germany. Tel: (0651) 201 2806-09. Fax: (0651) 201 3914.

CHECKLIST

1. How good is my German? Good enough for the environment in which I am going to live and work?

2. Can I do a course before going to Germany?

3. Do I have the time and money to spend a holiday in Germany? If yes, how can I make the best use of it?

4. Can I afford a language course in Germany? If yes, are there specialist classes for the sector in which I am going to work?

5. If I already have a job, would my employer sponsor a language course?

6. Would a work experience placement improve my job prospects? If yes, can I afford the time and money? For how long?

7. Could I improve my German by reading newspapers and magazines? If yes, which publications would interest me?

5
Finding a Job

LOOKING AT THE EMPLOYMENT SITUATION

The days when German companies were desperate to fill their vacancies
with foreign workers are over. But if you are patient, speak German and
are prepared to work hard, you can find temporary or permanent employment. In some sectors, for example nursing and construction, Germany still needs additional staff, and qualified foreign applicants are
encouraged. You can increase your chances by learning as much German as possible, including the terminology of your trade, and by gain-
ing work experience in Germany through voluntary work.

Be careful when accepting a job through an agency or direct from
an employer. Most job offers are honest and fair, but some ruthless
people rely on foreigners not understanding the legal situation or not
having the courage to go to court. It can happen that an employer
offers work to a foreigner who has no visa and cannot be employed
legally. The employer is aware of this, and simply doesn't pay wages.
After two or three months, when the worker demands payment, the
employers says the work was illegal and threatens that the worker will
be deported.

Although the employers risk being reported for this practice, they
usually get three months free labour from their illegal worker.

If you are in doubt about a job offer, consult the Arbeitsamt.

USING THE STATE EMPLOYMENT SERVICE

The Zentralstelle für Arbeitsvermittlung (Arbeitsamt for short) matches
applicants and vacancies. The service is free for both job-hunters and
employers. The Arbeitsamt is efficient, although can take many months
to find a placement for you, and you must remember that they can offer
you jobs only where there are vacancies.

If you are already in Germany, you can register with the nearest

Arbeitsamt branch. There is one in every city and in most medium and small towns. You may have to wait for an appointment.

Registering back home

You can also register while you are still in your home country. Get the necessary forms, and fill them in with your typewriter. Explain precisely the job(s) you are looking for. Your chances are better if you state 'bilingual secretary in import, export or transport business' than if you say you are looking for 'anything' or 'any office work'.

Address: Zentralstelle für Arbeitsvermittlung, Postfach 17 05 45, D-60079 Frankfurt, Germany. Tel: (069) 7111-0.

The Overseas Placing Unit

British residents should contact the Overseas Placing Unit (OPU) which offers advice and guidance for people who want to go abroad.

The Overseas Placing Unit liaises with the German Arbeitsamt, so you can save yourself complicated correspondence with the German authorities.

In addition, the OPU holds information on looking for work in specific trades and professions. Write to the OPU, giving details of the type of work you are looking for.

Job-hunters should approach their nearest job centre and ask for a search to be made of vacancies on the NATVACS (national vacancies) databank. The Overseas Placing Unit advertises all German vacancies on NATVACS.

However, the OPU deals only with vacancies in permanent or skilled work. If you are looking for seasonal and casual vacancies for unskilled work, such as fruit picking, you should contact the Zentralstelle für Arbeitsvermittlung in Frankfurt instead.

You can also apply speculatively for vacancies in Germany through the OPU. For this you have to complete two ES13 forms, one in English, one in German. The forms are available from local job centres or from the OPU.

Send the completed forms to the Overseas Placing Unit via the job centre with a CV, a covering letter, and copies of qualifications. The OPU forwards them to the Zentralstelle für Arbeitsvermittlung in Frankfurt.

Further details are in the booklets *Working Abroad* and *Working in Germany*, which are available from the nearest job centre as well as from the OPU.

Address: Overseas Placing Unit, Rockingham House, 123 West Street, Sheffield S1 4ER, UK. Tel: (01742) 596051. Fax: (01742) 596040.

USING EMPLOYMENT AGENCIES

The German law regarding recruitment agencies is much relaxed now, and job-hunters can register with agencies in Germany as well as with licensed agencies in other countries. Most agencies insist on seeing the candidates in person before including them in their files.

Recruitment agencies – except au pair agencies – may not charge you a fee for their services.

For addresses of German recruitment agencies, you can consult the *Germany Headhunters Guide* which costs £50. For those who aim at a particular geographical area, there are guides to the north and east, the south and the west, each with around 600 addresses, for £20 each.

Prices include postage; outside Europe an extra £2 is charged for airmail. Send for a free information leaflet initially to find out about current sizes and prices.

Address: Headhunters, Avotek Publishers, NL-6684 DL Ressen, Netherlands.

AVOIDING PITFALLS

In the past, foreigners have been exploited by certain international employment agencies. Workers paid the agencies for their services and arrived to find that their jobs did not exist. Or they worked for several months and never received payment. These cases have become rarer, but you should still be careful.

The Overseas Placing Unit suggests that UK residents get (for a small charge) a list of bona fide UK-based agencies which deal with work in Europe.

Address: The Federation of Recruitment and Employment Services, 36-38 Mortimer Street, London W1N 7RB, UK.

Ian Foulstone of the Overseas Placing Unit also recommends: 'If you accept work through an agency, ask to see their licence. They must have a licence from the government.' Good advice if you can read German and if you know what the licence should look like. Otherwise you may still be fooled.

The sharks work mostly in building and construction. If you are looking for work in this area and don't speak the language well, you are safer using the services of the Arbeitsamt.

Self-employment

Another problem is that many construction workers are lured into Germany with the promise of 'self-employed' contracts. These offers can be respectable. But to be self-employed in Germany, your qualifications and experiences must be the equivalent of, for example, a master bricklayer or master steel-fixer. This regulation is strictly enforced. If your qualifications are not up to this high standard, you cannot be self-employed.

You also need the form E101 from the Contributions Agency of the Department of Social Security. This form is only issued if you have been self-employed (not unemployed) in the UK before going to Germany.

LOOKING AT NEWSPAPER ADVERTISEMENTS

High-powered, well-paid positions are sometimes advertised in the daily newspapers outside Germany. For seasonal and au pair work, look at the newspaper *Overseas Jobs Express*, which sometimes carries advertisements for secretarial and computing vacancies too.

For 'jobs vacant' advertisements in German newspapers, look at the Saturday careers supplements. Unfortunately, the German dailies, when sold abroad, often don't carry these weekend supplements.

You can ask your friends in Germany to cut out job adverts which match your skill, but of course you have to be quick, so your application doesn't arrive much later than that of a native applicant.

National daily and weekly newspapers (such as *Frankfurter Allgemeine Zeitung* and *Die Zeit*) are the best source for well-paid, specialist positions. Employers who pay DM 80,000 or more a year for an employee will think an advertisement in a big paper is a worthwhile investment. It is also a matter of prestige for a company to advertise in the right papers.

Reply to advertisements in the national press only if you fit the description 100 per cent, as they can attract several hundred applications.

The chances are better with the regional daily newspapers, such as *Weserkurier, Süddeutsche Zeitung, Kölnische Rundschau, Schwäbische Zeitung, Stuttgarter Zeitung* or *Südkurier*. They are likely to carry situations vacant adverts for skilled tradespeople and secretaries.

Have a look at the trade magazines which cover your industry sector. If you don't know them already, look up their addresses in the reference library, either in *Willings Press Guide* or *Benn's Media Directory*.

How to read the adverts

Find out what your occupation is called in German. There may be more than one possible translation. The job title is printed in large, bold type in the advertisement, often followed by *'gesucht'* (wanted).

German law demands that both the female and the male version is printed, which results in lengthy words such as *'Kraftfahrzeugmechaniker/Kraftfahrzeugmechanikerin gesucht'* (car mechanic wanted). Others put the *'in'*, which shows the female version, in brackets or after a slash (for example, *'Kraftfahrzeugmechaniker/in gesucht'*) or put *'m/w'* (male/female) in brackets.

A salary range is sometimes, but not always, given. Many employers ask applicants to include their expectations in the letter: *'Bitte richten Sie Ihre Bewerbung mit Gehaltsvorstellung an . . .'*.

Some employers state which type of application they prefer. Watch out for the words *kurz* (short), *ausführlich* (detailed), *aussagefähig* (expressive), *handschriftlich* (handwritten), *vollständig* (complete).

A sentence which contains the word *'Kenntnisse'* or *'Fähigkeiten'* usually lists the required skills. They can be divided into *'Bedingung'* (a must) and *'von Vorteil'* (an advantage) or *'hilfreich'* (helpful). Watch out for *'Sprachkenntnisse'* (language skills) which are probably the ace up your sleeve.

The address at the end gives either a department (for example, *'Personalabteilung'*) or a person (for example, *'unsere Frau Schneider'*).

PLACING YOUR OWN ADVERTISEMENTS

The advertising rates in the national dailies are probably prohibitive unless you are confident you can recoup the money by getting a top-paying job.

Try the local and regional newspapers, and the trade press. If you know to which area you want to go, or the industry in which you want to work, you can find some addresses in *Willing's Press Guide* and *Benn's Media Directory*.

Use an address in your advertisement, if possible a German one. Perhaps your German friends would allow you to use theirs. German employers won't bother to reply to a box number advertisement.

Advertising prices are calculated by space (display) or by line

Chefsekretärin gesucht

Wir sind ein führender Hersteller und Exporteur von Spielwaren und Freizeitartikeln .

Für unseren Geschäftsführer suchen wir eine **erfahrene Sekretärin/ Assistentin** mit selbstsicherem Auftreten, Verhandlungsgeschick und Diplomatie. **Ausgezeichnete Englischkenntnisse**, mindestens fünf Jahre Sekretariatserfahrung und Computerkenntnisse sind Bedingung; weitere Sprachkenntnisse wären von Vorteil.

Bitte senden Sie Ihre ausführlichen Bewerbungsunterlagen mit Gehaltsvorstellung an unsere Personalabteilung.

Müller & Meier Spielwaren GmbH, Hauser Str. 1, Industriegebiet, 00000 Tupfingen.

PA wanted

We are a leading manufacturer and exporter of toys, games and leisure goods.

We are looking for an **experienced secretary/assistant** to our managing director. She must have self-confidence, negotiation skills and diplomacy. **Excellent English**, at least five years' secretarial experience and computing skills are essential. Additional languages would be an advantage.

Please send your detailed application dossier, including salary expectations, to our personnel department.

Müller & Meier Spielwaren GmbH, Hauser Str. 1, Industriegebiet, 00000 Tupfingen.

Fig. 3. Sample 'situations vacant' advertisement with translation.

(classified). Keep your text as short as possible to save money. Start with your occupation or qualification.

Ask the advertising department *(Anzeigenabteilung)* of the local or regional newspapers for advice on how to abbreviate your text to save costs without losing its meaning.

Sometimes you can choose between the full circulation area, and a part of it.

WRITING YOUR APPLICATION LETTER

Type your application on plain white A4 paper. Avoid coloured paper, but a faint yellowish or amber tint and good quality recycled paper are fine. Neat handwriting is accepted for non-office staff only.

What to Enclose

German employers judge the quality of an application by its volume. They expect your letter of application to be accompanied by:

1.   a detailed CV

2.   a passport-size portrait photo

3.   certificates of all schools you attended

4.   certificates of all exams you passed

5.   certificates of all courses you attended

6.   references from all previous employers.

Sometimes they also ask for additional references or samples of your handwriting.

Have a portrait photo taken and order many prints. For a senior position, you need good quality prints.

Don't send original documents; photocopies are acceptable. In the past, employers insisted that photocopies were certified by a police officer, a notary or a bank clerk. Luckily, this is no longer required.

WRITING A GERMAN-STYLE CV

Germans used to write long essay-style CVs, beginning with 'I was

Susan Smith
Südstr. 1
00000 Stadthausen
Telefon 0000/0000

1. Oktober 199X

Müller & Meier Spielwaren GmbH
Personalabteilung
Hauser Str. 1
Industriegebiet

00000-Tupfingen

Bewerbung

Sehr geehrte Damen und Herren,

mit Interesse habe ich Ihre Anzeige in der Samstagausgabe des "Stadtkurier" gelesen.

Ich bin eine erfahrene Fremdsprachensekretärin und habe mehrere Jahre als Abteilungssekretärin und als Chefassistentin gearbeitet. Englisch ist meine Muttersprache. Deutsch und Französisch beherrsche ich in Wort und Schrift. Ich bin mit allen Sekretariatsaufgaben, einschließlich Text-und Datenverarbeitung mit Computern, bestens vertraut.

Ich lebe seit einem Jahr in Deutschland. Ich suche eine verantwortungsvolle Stellung ab nächsten Monat, wenn mein derzeitiger Anstellungsvertrag, der auf ein Jahr befristet ist, ausläuft.

Meine Bewerbungsunterlagen liegen bei. Ich freue mich darauf, von Ihnen zu hören.

Mit freundlichen Grüßen

Susan Smith

Susan Smith

Anlagen
Lebenslauf
6 Zeugniskopien
Foto

Fig. 4. Sample application letter.

Susan Smith
Südstr. 1
00000 Stadthausen
Tel. 0000/0000

1 October 199X

Müller & Meier Spielwaren GmbH
Personalabteilung
Hauser Str. 1
Industriegebiet

00000-Tupfingen

Application

Dear Madams and Sirs,

I have read, with interest, your advertisement in the Saturday issue of
''Stadtkurier''.

I am an experienced bilingual secretary and I have worked as a group
secretary and personal assistant for several years. English is my mother
tongue, and I also speak and write fluent German and French. I am fully
familiar with all aspects of secretarial work, including word and data
processing.

I have lived in Germany for a year. I am looking for employment in a
responsible position, starting next month, when my current contract,
which is temporary for one year, will terminate.

I enclose my application dossier, and I look forward to hearing from you.

Yours faithfully,

Susan Smith

Susan Smith

Enclosures
CV
6 copies of certificates and references
Photo

Fig. 4. Sample application letter – translation.

born on . . . in . . . near . . . as the second son of (long list of titles and achievements, followed by name) . . . and his wife . . . (mentioning her and her father's names, titles and connections) in the village of . . . near . . . and mentioned every move the family made during childhood to another village or address.

If you find examples of such CVs in your German language textbook, beware. Today, employers prefer a concise CV *(Lebenslauf)*, usually typed.

The difference between a British and a German CV is that the German one is always arranged in chronological order. It lists your education first (from primary school to university), then your employment history (from your first job to your current occupation).

Differences to watch out for are figures. The Germans use a comma where the British use a full point, and a full point where the British use a comma. For example: 1,000,000 becomes 1.000.000, and 1.5 becomes 1,5.

The figures for seven and one differ from the British figures. Take care when a handwritten CV is required, and also when handwriting addresses, or your letters will be delivered to the wrong house. For one, write ⌐1, not 1. For seven, write ⁊, not 7.

German personnel managers want to know your hobbies to decide if you are a 'well-rounded' personality. Mention your hobbies, and include one intellectual interest (writing poetry, learning languages), one creative (painting, photography, pottery) and one type of sport, if possible a team sport with low accident risks.

WHAT TO TRANSLATE

Addresses – your own or your employers – should never be translated. Otherwise the reply will never arrive at the right address. However, you may want to add the international dialling code to make it easier for a German employer to contact you in your home country.

It is important that your prospective employer, who may only speak German, understands your experience and skills. But few job titles and qualifications have an exact equivalent in German. A possible solution is to give job titles and qualifications in your native language, but add a brief translation, and explanation if necessary, in brackets.

Skills are measured in different ways in Germany. Shorthand speed is calculated in syllables per minute and typing in letters per minute. If you know your typing speed in words per minute, multiply it by five, and you get your approximate typing speed in letters per minute.

VOLUNTARY AND AU PAIR WORK

If you want to work in Germany mainly to widen your horizon, improve your language skills or gain experience in a new field, and if income and living standard are not important, consider doing voluntary or au pair work.

Volunteering

There are several organisations offering postings in Germany. Food and accommodation are usually provided, but you have to arrange and pay for your travel to Germany and back. Some organisations pay pocket money, other expect volunteers to contribute towards the expenses of the project.

Aktion Sühnezeichen

You work on projects which promote peace and protect minorities, in return for free board and lodging, and DM 250 pocket money a month. You must be 18 years or over, have work experience in a social institution in your home country, and commit yourself for at least eighteen months. Applicants are selected during a seminar.

Address: Aktion Sühnezeichen Friedensdienste e.V., Postfach 154, D-10365 Berlin, Germany. Tel: (030) 55190310. Fax: (030) 55190376.

Christlicher Friendensdienst

Three or four weeks unpaid work experience in work camps. Projects include social work with children and nature conservation. Volunteers must be 18-26 years. The projects are suitable for handicapped people. Accommodation in dormitories is provided.

Address: CFD, Christlicher Friedensdienst, Rendelerstr. 9-11, D-60385 Frankfurt, Germany. Tel: (069) 459072. Fax: (069) 461213.

Applicants from the UK can apply to the British branch:

Address: Christian Movement for Peace, 186 St Paul's Road, Balsall Heath, Birmingham B12 8LZ, UK. Tel: (0121) 4465704. Fax: (0421) 4464060.

Freiwilliges Soziales Jahr

Volunteers between 17 and 25 can apply for one-year placements in hospitals, children's or old people's homes, and homes for the physically or mentally handicapped. You get hospital canteen meals, accommodation in twin-bedded rooms, about DM 300 per month pocket money, and on-the-job training in nursing duties.

The brochure *ABC zum Diakonischen Jahr* gives detailed information about the project, and lists addresses of institutions which accept volunteers.

Address: Arbeitskreis Freiwillige Soziale Dienste, Stafflenbergstr. 76, D-70184 Stuttgart, Germany. Tel: (0711) 2159-0. Fax: (0711) 2159-288.

Main organisers for Freiwilliges Soziales Jahr include:

Arbeiterwohlfahrt (Worker's Charity), Oppelner Str. 130, D-53119, Bonn, Germany.

Bund der Deutschen Katholischen Jugend (Catholic Youth Association), Carl-Mosters-Platz 1, D-40477 Düsseldorf, Germany.

Deutsches Rotes Kreuz (German Red Cross), Friedrich-Ebert-Allee 71, D-53113 Bonn, Germany.

Spending a year au pair

As an au pair, you contribute five hours a day household and child care work in return for pocket money, one full day off a week, and the opportunity to attend language classes. You may have to babysit for two nights a week. You get your own, lockable room, but you have to make and pay for your own travel arrangements.

Au pairing is suitable for people between 18 and 27 who have some experience in either housework (for example, can cook simple meals) or child care (for example, have done some babysitting).

You can apply through agencies either in your home country or in Germany. Addresses include:

Solihull Au Pair & Nanny Agency, Debbie Bushell, 1565 Stratford Road, Hall Green, Birmingham B28 9JA, UK. Tel: (0121) 733 6444. Fax: (0121) 733 6555.

South Eastern Au Pair Bureau, Sandra Clark, 39 Rutland Avenue, Thorpe Bay, Essex SS1 2XJ, UK. Tel: (01702) 601911.

You can get further addresses from the German National Tourist Office in your home country.

TEMP AND VACATION JOBS

Popular short-term jobs include waiter or waitress (except in university towns where the students compete for the jobs), trade fair hostessing (for multilingual females), fruit and grape harvesting. You can find them through your own initiative, or register with the nearest Arbeitsamt.

CASE STUDIES

Claire's surprise interview
'I filled in the form ES13 from the Overseas Placing Unit, asking for a long-term temporary position as a bilingual secretary in Germany. I didn't hear anything back, and almost forgot about it. Then, after six months, I received a job description, compiled by the Arbeitsamt. A bank in Frankfurt was looking for a bilingual secretary with English mother tongue. Then everything happened quickly. I sent my application dossier, and was invited for an interview. A week later I was told I had the job and could start in two months' time.'

Sarah gets the job
'There was a notice on our Sixth Form common room door, saying that an au pair was required in Heusenstamm, the German twin town of Tonbridge where my school was. I ignored it at first thinking I would never get the job because I didn't speak a word of German. But the notice remained, nobody else had applied. I decided to apply and was accepted. I didn't realise what I was doing until I was waiting in the car queue at Dover.'

Kevin takes a chance
'I saw an advertisement in a newspaper. An agency was recruiting bricklayers for Germany. I applied, was accepted, packed my suitcase and went. Thinking back, I was rather naive. I didn't check the agency's credentials or ask for a contract. I was just happy to escape unemployment.

'The employer delayed paying my wages, saying that I would receive the outstanding money once the three-month trial period was over, because of the complicated German tax law. I was annoyed but not suspicious. What did I know about German legislation? Then, after three months, he fired me. I was too scared and confused to take him to a German court.

'I registered with the Arbeitsamt, but by now it was December and not many building jobs around. Then the authorities caught up with me, saying the period I could stay as a tourist was over, and I was not employed. I could not prove that I had been employed for the first three months, because the builder denied it.

'By chance I met someone whose mother was a retail manager. She needed someone to step in for a warehouse worker who had broken his arm, just before Christmas, when there was a lot of work. I was available immediately and got the job. It was well-paid, but lasted only for two weeks. At least that solved the problem with the German authorities for a while.

'A few weeks later, the Arbeitsamt got me a job in eastern Germany, on a six-month contract. I'm not earning as much as I had hoped, less than my German colleagues, but more than the workers from the eastern European countries. Certainly more than if I was unemployed in the UK. My employer is pleased with my work. He says that he'll probably renew my contract, and if I learn to speak more German, he'll give me German wages.'

USEFUL WORDS AND PHRASES

Abendkurs/Abendschule evening classes
Adresse address
Anlage(n) enclosure(s)
Anzeige/Inserat advertisement
Anzeigenabteilung advertising department
Arbeitgeber employer
Arbeitsvermittlungsagentur recruitment agency
ausführlich detailed
aussagefähig expressive
baldmöglichst/zum nachstmöglichen Termin as soon as possible
Berufsausbildung/Lehre training, apprenticeship
Berufserfahrung professional/work experience
Bewerbung application
Bewerbungsbrief/Bewerbungsschreiben letter of application
Bewerbungsunterlagen complete dossier with letter, CV, copies of references and certificates, photo
Bitte richten Sie Ihre Bewerbung an please address your application to (followed by name or department)
Chiffre box number
Fähigkeiten skills

Familienstand marital status
fließend fluent
freiwilling voluntary
Geburtsdatum date of birth
Geburtsort place of birth
Genehmigung licence
Gehaltsvorstellung salary expectations
geschieden divorced
gesucht wanted
getrennt lebend separated
Grundschule primary school
handschriftlich handwritten
Hobbys hobbies
Ich bin interessiert an I am interested in
Ich freue mich darauf, von Ihnen zu hören I look forward to hearing from you
Kenntnisse knowledge, skills
Kleinanzeige classified advertisement
kurz short
Kurzschrift/Stenografie shorthand
Lebenslauf CV
Maschinenschreiben typing
Mit freundlichen Grüßen Yours sincerely/Yours faithfully
mit Interesse with interest
Nachname surname
Name name
Postleitzahl post code
Qualifikation(en) qualification(s)
Referenzen references
Schulbildung school or college education
Sehr geehrte Daman und Herren Dear Madams and Sirs
Sprachkenntnisse language skills
Staatsangehörigkeit nationality
Stelle vacancy
Stellenangebot(e) situations vacant advertisement(s)
Stellengesuch(e) jobs wanted advertisement(s)
Studium university studies
tabellarisch tabular
Telefon, Telefonnummer telephone
Textverarbeitung word processing
unverheiratet/ledig single

verheiratet   married
ver witwet   widowed
vollständig   complete
Vorname(n)   first, Christian name(s)
Vorstellungsgespräch   interview
Vorwahl   area code
Wegen Erweiterung. . ./Zum Ausbau. . .   indication that business is
   expanding
Weitere Informationen   additional information
Weiterführende Schule(n)   secondary school(s)
Wohnort   town, village of residence
Zeugnis(se)   reference(s)/certificate(s)
Zeitarbeit   temporary work

6
Handling the Paperwork

The Germans believe in doing everything correctly and in an established order. This means a lot of paperwork. Be prepared to fill in many forms throughout your stay, especially during the first few months. Don't skip essential registration formalities. German employers, landlords, professional associations all may require proof that you have registered.

VISAS, RESIDENCE AND WORK PERMITS

The leaflet *Residence and Work in Germany*, available from the German embassy in London, currently contains the information summarised below. Remember that rules and regulations may change. Send for the latest version before you commit yourself.

Address: Deutsche Botschaft/German Embassy, 23 Belgrave Square, London SW1X 8PZ, UK. Tel: (0171) 235 5033.

European Union nationals
If you are a national of a European Union country and want to look for work or become self-employed in Germany, you don't need a visa or a work permit to enter the country. You can also take your spouse and children (up to the age of 21) with you. You need a valid passport or an official identity card.

Once you are in Germany, you and your family must obtain a residence permit. This must be after you have taken up employment, but before you have spent three months in the country.

This means that you can spend up to three months job hunting without much official paperwork. However, you will not get a residence permit if you don't have a job within three months. It can be a good idea to take any temporary job that comes up within the first three months, apply for a residence permit, and later look for permanent or more satisfying employment.

If you plan to live in Germany, but not to work there – for example, to work on a research project of your own – you can still get a residence permit. In this case you must prove that you have enough money to live in Germany, that you have accommodation and that you are covered by medical insurance. You apply for the residence permit as soon as possible after arriving in Germany.

You get the residence permit at the nearest Ausländeramt, see below.

Nationals of other countries

At present, all non-EU nationals need a visa if they want to live and work in Germany. You have to apply before you go to Germany.

You can obtain the application forms from the Visa Section of the German Embassy in your home country. When you submit the filled in forms, you must enclose a valid passport, two passport photographs, a written confirmation of the employer that you have a job in Germany, and proof of medical insurance cover in Germany.

If the visa is granted, you can enter Germany, where the relevant Ausländeramt will issue your residence permit.

The procedure is easier if you are a national of Finland, Iceland, Liechtenstein, Norway, Switzerland and the USA. You can apply for the residence and work permit after entry into Germany.

REGISTRATION

When you take up residence in Germany, you must register with the local Einwohnermeldeamt (registry office), within one week. Take your passport with you.

You receive three copies of the registration form. One you have to take to your new landlord/landlady in Germany, get it countersigned by them, and return it to the Einwohnermeldeamt. This should present no problems. Another one is supposed to be countersigned by your previous landlord/landlady at your former place of residence. The authorities are not likely to make much fuss about this if your last residence was outside Germany.

Each time you move to another area, you must de-register with one Einwohnermeldeamt and re-register with another one, and each time you must have the forms countersigned by the previous and the new landlord.

RESIDENCE PERMITS

To apply for a residence permit, you go to the Ausländeramt (foreign nationals authority). Remember to take documents with you which prove that you have employment already or are going to take up employment (for example, a contract or a letter from your employer). You must also prove that you have a permanent place to live in, and take three passport photographs. You will get a five-year Aufenthaltsgenehmigung (residence permit).

The Ausländerbehörde is usually based at the Rathaus (town hall) or at the Kreisverwaltung (area administration centre).

Getting an extension

If you don't find a job immediately, you may get a two-month extension to the initial three months, but you must prove that you have the money to survive for two months (take a bank statement). Apply for the extension before your three-month period has run out or you may get into trouble. You must find a job within these two months.

The time factor

Remember that everything official in Germany involves much waiting, form-filling, and getting stamps and signatures from this office and that authority. This can be time-consuming. If you have a job already, arrive in Germany at least one week before you start working, to have enough time for all the red tape. Once you have taken up work, your employer will not be pleased if you need time off.

SOCIAL SECURITY, HEALTH AND INSURANCE

Paying your social security contributions

Your employer deducts your social security contributions at source, and transfers them, with the employer's share, to the relevant pension, health and unemployment funds.

Certain jobs are *sozialversicherungsfrei*, which means that you don't have to pay social security contributions, and you get your gross wages as net wages, because the employer pays the tax. However, you won't get any contributions towards a pension fund. Jobs which pay less than DM 580 per month fall into this category. However, the limit changes often, so get up-to-date information before signing a contract.

At the end of the year, your employer gives you a slip of paper which shows the contributions paid on your behalf to the pension scheme. Check every five years or so what your pension claim is and if you have all documents complete.

Choosing your healthcare

You can choose with which Krankenkasse (health insurance fund) you want to register. Some cater only for specific professions or industries. These are called Ersatzkassen (for example, DAK, KKH, Barmer Ersatzkasse, Techniker Krankenkasse), others are open to everyone (such as the Allgemeine Ortskrankenkasse, AOK for short). Ersatzkassen may be cheaper than the AOK, but the AOK has more branches.

Your employers appreciate it if you choose a Krankenkasse to which other members of staff already belong, as it will keep their amount of paperwork down. You may want to let your employers' personnel department select and sort out your Krankenkasse for you. They can get and fill in the forms for you, and all you have to do is sign.

Otherwise, choose your Krankenkasse as soon as you accept a job. You must register with one, unless your income is in the higher brackets, in which case you can opt for private health insurance instead.

The Krankenkasse gives a membership card which looks like a credit card. Each time you visit a GP, specialist or dentist, you hand the card to the receptionist or surgery assistant who handles the administration with your Krankenkasse.

To find the best Krankenkasse for you, check:

● Is the branch near where I live or where I work?

● Are its opening hours convenient?

● Are other members of staff registered with the same Krankenkasse?

● What are the monthly contributions?

● Does the Krankenkasse pay towards spectacles and dentures? How much?

Here are the addresses of some major Krankenkasse:

DKV Deutsche Krankenversicherung AG, Aachener Str. 300, D-50933 Köln, Germany. Tel: (0221) 578-0. Fax: (0221) 5783694.
DAK, Deutsche Angestellten-Krankenkasse, D-20097 Hamburg, Nagelsweg 27-35, Germany. Tel: (040) 23961271. Fax: (040) 23962120.

KKH, Kaufmännische Krankenkasse, Indenburgstr. 43-45, D-30175 Hannover, Germany. Tel: (0511) 2802-213. Fax: (0511) 2802-232.

Techniker Krankenkasse, Hauptverwaltung, Bramfelder Str. 140, D-22305 Hamburg, Germany.

AOK Bundesverband, Kortrijker Str. 1, D-53177 Bonn, Germany. Tel: (0228) 843-309. Fax: (0228) 843 507.

Immunisation

You don't need any vaccinations for Germany, unless you come from an area where there is an outbreak of a dangerous infectious disease. But remember to take your vaccination record with you, so your German GP can see if and when the immunisations need updating.

Insurance

You may decide to take out additional insurance:

- A supplementary health insurance which pays for first class hospital treatment.

- Accident insurance (*Unfallversicherung*).

- Personal liability insurance (*Haftpflichtversicherung*).

- A private pension scheme (*private Rentenversicherung*).

- Life insurance (*Lebensversicherung*).

- Motoring third party insurance (*Kfz-Haftpflicht-Versicherung*, obligatory if you have a car).

- Voluntary fire, theft and comprehensive insurance (*Kaskoversicherung*) for your car.

You find insurance brokers and offices in every town, and can look them up in the *Gelbe Seiten* (Yellow Pages equivalent). Choose an insurance company which your friends or neighbours recommend.

One major insurance company is: DBV, Zentraldirektion, Frankfurter Str. 50, D-65178 Wiesbaden, Germany. Tel: (0611) 363-0.

PAYING TAXES

Your income tax (*Lohnsteuer* or *Einkommensteuer*), as well as the church tax if you belong to the Roman Catholic or Protestant church, is also deducted at source. The tax scale increases proportionally to your income. Income tax is between 22 and 53 per cent of your income. For details, contact the nearest Finanzamt (tax office).

As soon as you accept a job offer, you must get a *Lohnsteuerkarte* (income tax card) from the Einwohnermeldeamt, and give it to your employer's personnel department.

Getting a refund

You may be eligible for a tax refund at the end of the year. For this, you have to fill in a *Lohnsteuerjahresausgleich* (annual adjustment of income tax) form. You have a good chance of getting a refund if you have spent some of your income on job- or career-related training courses and materials. Keep all receipts, and use the services of a *Steuerberater* (tax consultant) if necessary.

Church tax

You can avoid paying church tax (which can amount to several hundred DM a year) if you declare that you don't belong to a church. It is best to make this declaration when you register with the Einwohnermeldeamt. If you decide to leave the church later, the authorities will charge a substantial handling fee.

Before you decide to give up church membership, remember that this may lower your respectability in the eyes of some conservative employers. You may also face unwanted difficulties in having your children baptised, or you may find the only kindergarten available is run by a church and Christian children are given priority. Last but not least, search your conscience. The churches depend on the taxes as their main source of income.

BANKING

If you have a permanent job, your employer will pay your wages direct into your bank account. To open an account, go to a bank and pay in a small sum, usually DM 10 or 20.

The account you need is a *Gehaltskonto* (current account). Ask for a cheque-book, as well as for eurocheques. In addition, you may want to have a *Sparbuch* (savings account).

If you plan to transfer money regularly from Germany to your home country or vice versa, find out how long it takes and how much it costs. The costs may be prohibitive. The cheapest way if to take with you as much money in cash as safety permits whenever you travel.

If you plan to spend money from your UK (or other European country) bank account often while in Germany, the best solution is to use eurocheques, which are popular in Germany and accepted almost everywhere.

Contacts
For further information, contact the following banking organisations:

Deutsche Bundesbank, Wilhelm-Epstein-Str. 14, D-60431 Frankfurt, Germany. Tel: (069) 95661. Fax: (069) 5601071.

Deutscher Sparkassen- und Girobank e.V., Simrockstr. 4, D-53113 Bonn, Germany. Tel: (0228) 2040. Fax: (0228) 204250.

Deutsche Girozentrale, Deutsche Kommunalbank e.V., Postfach 110542, D-60040 Frankfurt, Germany. Tel: (069) 26930. Fax: (069) 2693490.

Bundesverband der Deutschen Volksbanken und Raiffeisenbanken e.V., Postfach 1204, D-53046 Bonn, Germany. Tel: (0228) 5090. Fax: (0228) 509201.

Bundesverband Deutscher Banken e.V., Kattenburg 1, D-50667 Köln, Germany. Tel: (0221) 16630. Fax: (0221) 166322.

USEFUL WORDS AND PHRASES

Anmeldung   registration
Ausländeramt   foreign nationals authority
Bankkonto   bank account
Einkommensteuer   income tax
Einwohnermeldeamt   registry office
Finanzamt   tax office
Gehaltskonto   current account (for wages)
Kirchensteuer   church tax
Krankenkasse   public health insurance
Krankenversicherung   health insurance
Lohnsteuer   income tax
private Versicherung   private insurance
Rentenversicherung   pension scheme
Scheckbuch   cheque-book
Sparbuch   savings account

Steuer   tax
Unfallversicherung   accident insurance
Versicherung   insurance

CHECKLIST

Between arriving and taking up work, you should have accomplished a considerable amount of paperwork. Use this checklist to make sure you haven't forgotten anything essential.

1.   Have I registered with the Einwohnermeldeamt?

2.   Have I registered with the Ausländeramt?

3.   Have I registered with a church (if applicable)? Ask at the Einwohnermeldeamt for details. If you register, you will have to pay church taxes.

4.   Have I registered with a Krankenkasse, or arranged private health insurance cover?

5.   Have I opened a bank account?

6.   Have I obtained a Lohnsteuerkarte?

7.   Do I have an employment contract?

7
Finding Accommodation

FLAT-HUNTING

One of the difficulties of living in Germany is finding accommodation. Most Germans rent, rather than buy, a house or a flat, and there are more would-be tenants than dwellings.

The situation is worst in the cities, especially in München (Munich) and Berlin. If you work in a city, you may have to commute over long distances.

What it costs

The size of the village, town or city, as well as the wealth of the area, determines the price. Expect to pay DM 14 a square metre (excluding bills) for a flat in a big town. In a comparatively wealthy town, such as Konstanz, a flat with three rooms costs at least DM 1,000 per month (excluding bills). In Villingen, a town of similar size and in the same Bundesland, you may get one for DM 600. Expect to pay less in a village, and much more in a city.

The time it takes

Flat-hunting can become a full-time occupation for several months, and may turn into a nightmare. Buy the local daily newspaper which carries a classified section once a week. You'll notice that the '*Mietgesuche*' (accommodation wanted) columns take up ten times as much space as the '*Zu vermieten*' (accommodation offered). Whenever you pick up the phone to enquire about an advertised flat, you are told that it's gone. And if you are lucky enough to be invited to view a place, chances are that fifty competitors are already there.

If you are invited to view a flat, dress smartly and look as respectable as possible. Be prepared to put down the deposit on the spot if you like the place. If you don't, someone else will.

Sometimes it's the present tenants who are looking for successors

Zu vermieten

1-Zi.-Whg

Tupfingen, ca. 35m^2

Wohnfläche, sep. kl.

Küche, gr. Balkon, m.

Keller, Garage, ab sof.

DM 700,- plus

Nebenkosten u. Kaution

Immobilien Schmidt,

Tel 00000/0000

Zimmer in Tupfingen

möbl., an Student/in, NR, zu vermieten. Bad- u. Küchenmitbenutzung. Nähe Stadtzentrum. DM 400,- warm.

Tel. 0000/0000 (nach 18.00 Uhr)

Zu vermieten

3-Zi-Whg, EG, Südlage, 86qm,

Keller- u. Waschmasch.-Mitbenutzung., kl. Garten,

Nähe Uni u. Bahnhof, WG-geeignet.

Tel. 00000/0000

To let

Studio flat

in Tupfingen, approx. 35

sq. m. living area,

with small separate

kitchen, large balcony,

cellar, garage, immediate

vacancy, DM 700,-

plus bills and deposit

Immobilien Schmidt

(agent),

Tel. 00000/0000

Room in Tupfingen

furnished, to let to student (non-smoking). Share kitchen, bath. Near town centre. DM 400.- incl heating bills.

Tel. 0000/0000 (after 6pm)

To let

Flat with three rooms, ground floor, south facing, 86 sq. m., share cellar and washing machine, small garden, near university and station, suitable for flatshare.

Tel. 00000/0000

Fig. 5. 'Accommodation vacant' advertisements with translation.

('*Nachmieter*'). In return for recommending you to the landlord, they may demand payment for *Ablöse* or *Abstand*. Demanding such bribes is against the law and is therefore disguised as compensation for furniture left behind. If the present tenant suggests that you pay DM 1,500 for a couple of faded curtains, they are suggesting you bribe them to this amount.

Using an agent

A *Makler* (agent) usually charges a fee equivalent to two months' rent. Properties registered with agents are likely to be expensive. Agents, too, have long waiting-lists of prospective tenants and cannot guarantee to find a place within a few weeks or months. They are not allowed to charge for registration; you pay them only for their success.

Placing an advert

The best method is probably to place your own advertisement in the classified section of your local newspaper. Describe yourself as a professional, quiet, non-smoking woman without pets (or whatever).

Mention your job, and perhaps the name of your employer, as well as the type of accommodation you are looking for, the preferred district, and the rent you're willing to pay. Always give a telephone number; if necessary, that of a friend in Germany. Landlords are unlikely to respond to box numbers.

You can ask your employer to place an advert for you: '*Wir suchen für unsere Dolmetscherin eine Zwei-Zimmer-Wohnung. . .*' (We are looking for a two-room flat for our interpreter. . .). Many landlords respond to this type of advertisement, because it shows that you are *seriös* (respectable). However, the resulting offers may be slightly overpriced.

The best heading for a flat-wanted advert is *Belohnung* (reward). Although demanding bribes is illegal, offering bribes is not! The amount offered varies, usually one month's rent; compare other advertisements. That's still cheaper than using a *Makler*.

If the practice of bribing repells you, or if you cannot afford it, take an original approach. Offer a non-material reward. One flat-hunter had astonishing success by offering a home-baked apple cake. What could you offer?

Other ways of finding a flat

Put up cards with 'flat wanted/reward offered' headings at the noticeboards in universities, polytechnics, colleges, shops and pubs which are frequented by students.

Mietgesuche

Zimmer gesucht

Sekretärin, ruhig, seriös, NR, sucht Zimmer, auch in WG, od. kl. Whg, bis DM 650,- warm. Ab sofort für ein Jahr. Tel. 0000/0000

Einen großen Blumenstrauß...

für die erfolgreiche Vermittlung einer 3-Zi-Whg in zentr. Lage, mögl. m. Garten, für jg. Paar m. Kind. Bis DM 1.300 Kaltmiete. Tel. 0000/0000 (tags, Klaus)

Accommodation wanted

Room wanted

Secretary, quiet, respectable, non-smoking, wants room (flatshare considered) or small flat, maximum rent DM 650.- incl. bills. Tel. 0000/00000

A large bunch of flowers...

for the person who is successful in finding a flat with three rooms in central situation, if possible with garden, for a young couple with child. Rent up to DM 1,300.- plus bills. Tel. 0000/0000 (during daytime only, ask for Klaus)

Fig. 6. 'Accommodation wanted' advertisements with translation.

Contact the local *Mitwohnzentrale*, if there is one in your town. This means 'accommodation share centre' and is a business, sometimes run by students, which charges lower fees than normal agents. It specialises in finding tenants for flatshares.

It also finds subtenants if the main tenant goes on holiday for a few weeks. The Mitwohnzentrale takes up references and gives advice on a subletting contract. The main tenants know that their plants will be watered, the cats fed, the post forwarded, the rooms heated if there is danger of frost, and that the place is not deserted to tempt burglars. The subtenant gets accommodation at a reasonable price, paying only the rent and the bills, or even less.

Applying as a subtenant through a Mitwohnzentrale is ideal if you plan to explore several areas of Germany, living and working for a few weeks in each place, or if you need temporary accommodation until you find something permanent.

Holiday accommodation

In tourist areas, especially around the lakes, you can rent holiday accommodation during winter at a reasonable price. If you stay in Germany during the summer holidays, you may be able to get a room in a *Studentenwohnheim* (university hall).

Other possibilities include the Christlicher Verein junger Menschen (CVJM = YMCA) and Jugendherbergen (youth hostels).

In a Jugendherberge, you sleep in rooms with two to six beds. Women and men are strictly separated. You will not find much privacy, and the early closing time (you may have to be in by 10 p.m.) may make your social life difficult. In addition, you must not stay more than a few days in each hostel.

On the other hand, the accommodation is clean and reasonably priced, and perfect for working travellers. Germany has about 700 youth hostels. A booklet with addresses costs DM 6.50. You need a membership card, which you can get from the youth hostel association in your home country. Book your place in advance and in writing, and remember that in Bavaria, visitors must be under 27 years.

Signing your contract

Flat-letting contracts are detailed. If your landlord doesn't provide one, buy a standard form at the newsagents. Some landlords try to insert unacceptable clauses: no showering after 10 p.m., no male visitors, no pets. Check before you sign.

The clauses for the period of notice can be tricky in Germany: you can give notice only to certain dates, for example the last day of the month, with a period of several weeks.

Tenants are responsible for any repairs for which in the UK the landlord would pay, and have to redecorate the property completely when they move out.

If you meet the previous tenants before you move in, discuss the possibility that you do the redecorating if they pay for the materials. They will probably be glad not having to bother, and you get the wallpaper and paints you like. Remember to inform the landlord of this arrangement.

BUYING A PLACE

Few people in Germany buy their own place, but it is possible to acquire a house or a flat. You can use an agent. It may be easier to find property to buy than to rent. But when you decide to move on, you will have difficulty in selling it, because there are few prospective buyers.

In Britain people tend to buy their first property when they are young, then trade it in for a larger place, and finally sell their house when they reach retirement age, rent a small place and spend the money. In Germany, they live in rented accommodation while they are young, and perhaps save up money to buy their own place when they retire.

FURNISHING YOUR FLAT

Rooms and bedsits are usually let furnished, flats and houses unfurnished. Unfurnished flats may have a built-in kitchen.

You can buy furniture at a *Möbelhaus* (furniture store) or from a *Versandhandel* (mail order firm). If you want to buy second-hand furniture, perhaps because you don't plan to stay for a long time, read the classified advertisements in the local newspaper. There are often good bargains.

Better still, ask if the previous tenants are willing to sell any of the furniture, curtains and household items they are not taking at a cheap price. This is a normal arrangement.

if you plan to renovate, restore, decorate or furnish a house or flat, you can get ideas and addresses from the magazine *Das Haus*. For details, see page 119.

What's different

German houses don't normally have fireplaces, neither for real log fires nor for electric or gas substitutes. Heating is either by *Zentralheizung* (central heating) or by *Ölofen* (oil heater). Gas and electricity are sometimes used.

German furnishing and decorating styles depend on fashion and taste, but on the whole the Germans use plainer fabrics and fewer patterns. For wallpaper, woodchip paper is popular – lasts for ages and can be painted in a different shade each time the owner fancies a change.

Britons are often surprised to see the Germans put their name-plate on the entrance door, next to the doorbell. This is customary, and you are expected to do the same. Everyone would assume that something fishy is going on behind the door without a name-plate.

For security reasons, put only your surname, without initials, on the name-plate.

Many German houses have a cellar, and if you rent a flat, you may be granted a share of it. Use it to store fruit and vegetables, or put your washing-machine there.

BUYING HOUSEHOLD EQUIPMENT

To buy new household equipment, such as saucepans, cutlery and crockery, you can go to a *Haushaltswarengeschäft* (hardware store), an *Elektrowarenfachhandel* (electric appliances shop) or a *Kaufhaus* (supermarket).

Electric appliances run on 220 volts, and it is best to buy them locally. However, you can buy adaptors to use any small electric item you have brought from home. Appliances made in Germany are probably the best and most reliable, although some foreign makes are cheaper.

Equipment used in Germany is the same as in other European countries. However, the Germans are fond of fondue, so you may want to buy a fondue set to entertain guests. Tea kettles are less common than in the UK; the Germans prefer to brew ground coffee in a proper coffee machine.

A washing-machine is essential as there are few launderettes in Germany, and those that exist charge prohibitive rates.

Picking up second-hand bargains for household items is difficult. There are no charity shops in Germany, no jumble sales, and few car boot sales. Check the classified section of the local newspaper for a *Haushaltsauflösung*. This is the equivalent of a garage sale and is organised when someone has died or is moving house.

CASE STUDY

Claire goes flat-hunting

'Finding a flat was more difficult than finding the job. In Frankfurt, the rents were too high, and in the surrounding area people were suspicious of a single mother. At first we lived in a furnished holiday apartment, but this was available for the winter months only, and expensive.

'An American colleague and I considered sharing a flat. By chance we attended a local wine festival, and shared a table with a couple who had a flat to let. That's where the three of us are living now.

'Curtains are important. Especially in rural areas, your neighbours would be scandalised if you didn't have curtains and nets. We couldn't believe it. At every opportunity, our neighbours asked us if our curtains had arrived yet. We told them we didn't want curtains, and that we thought our roller blinds were much nicer. Then one day, they sent a delegation with all the old curtains and nets the neighbourhood could spare. They thought we were obviously too poor to buy curtains. Leaving windows without curtains was the equivalent of going out naked in the streets.'

ADDRESSES

Deutsches Jugendherbergswerk, Hauptverband e.V., Bismarckstr. 8, Postfach 20, D-32754 Detmold, Germany. Tel: (052 31) 74010. Fax: (0531) 640149.

CVJM Gesamtverband Deutschland, Postfach 410149, Im Druseltal 8, D-34131 Kassel-Wilhelmshöhe, Germany.

USEFUL WORDS AND PHRASES

Ablöse, Abstand   payment to former tenant
Belohnung   reward
Besteck   cutlery
Bett   bed
Drei-Zimmer-Wohnung (3 Zi Whg)   flat with three rooms plus bath and kitchen
Einbauküche   built-in kitchen
Erdgeschoß   ground floor
Haus   house
Haustür   entrance door

Herd cooker
Jugendherberge youth hostel
Kaffeemaschine coffee maker
Kaltmiete rent excluding bills
Kaution deposit
Keller cellar
Kochtopf saucepan
Kühlschrank refrigerator
Mieter/Mieterin tenant
Möbel furniture
Möbelhaus furniture store
möbliert furnished
Nachmieter gesucht successor wanted (willing to pay *Ablöse* to present tenant)
Nebenkosten (NK) bills
Nichtraucher/Nichtraucherin (NR) non-smoker
Provision agent's fee
ruhig quiet (used for flats and tenants alike)
Schlafsaal dormitory
Speicher attic
Studentenwohnheim university hall
teilmöbliert part furnished
Teppich carpet
unmöbliert unfurnished
Untermieter/Untermieterin subtenant
Vermieter/Vermieterin landlord, landlady
Versandhandel mail order firm
Vorhänge curtains
Waschmaschine washing-machine
Wohngemeinschaft (WG) flatshare
Wohnung (Whg) flat
Wohnung gesucht flat wanted
zentrale Lage central location
Zentralheizung (ZH) central heating
Zimmer room
Zimmer mit Frühstück bed and breakfast
Zu vermieten to let

8
Working in Germany

SIGNING YOUR CONTRACT

The employment contract, signed by both you and your employer, is called *Arbeitsvertrag* for workers, *Anstellungsvertrag* for employees and *Ausbildungsvertrag* for trainees and apprentices.

It can comprise just a few sentences, but Germans prefer documents which are several pages long. Check that the following points are covered to your satisfaction:

- your job title and a description of your duties
- your gross monthly salary
- indication if there is a 13th or 14th salary
- your annual leave entitlement
- the period of notice
- a trial period.

GETTING PAID

Most workers and employees are paid monthly, but there are some whose wages are calculated per hour, per day or per week. Women are still at a disadvantage and get paid less than men doing similar jobs.

In the eastern part of Germany, wages are on average much lower than in the west, but it is expected that this situation will change soon. For example, in 1993, workers in the east earned on average DM 35,569 a year, which is 64.6 per cent of what a worker in the west was paid. The average employee in the trade, banking and insurance industries earned DM 41,904 a year in the east and DM 60,871 in the west.

Salaries are usually paid monthly. When negotiating payment, discuss it in terms of DM a month. Ask if there will be a *Dreizehntes Monatsgehalt* (thirteenth monthly salary). This is a bonus for staff who remain with an employer for a year or more. If you complete one year, you get paid for thirteen months instead of twelve. Part of this extra payment is made before you take your summer holidays, the rest before Christmas.

In some sectors, even a fourteenth monthly salary is possible. In this case, you get a full month's salary in summer and another one in winter.

Collective agreements

If your contract contains the clause *'Bezahlung nach Tarif'*, this means that you will be paid according to the collective agreement between the employers and trade unions. On the whole, this is a good thing. You know that you get paid fairly, and whenever trade unions and employers' organisations negotiate and increase, you receive more money without bargaining yourself, even if you don't belong to a union. Ask your trade union, or your employer, for a copy for the current *Tarifvertrag* (collective pay agreement).

JOINING A TRADE UNION

Germany's workforce comprises 35.5 million people. About half the German population think that trade unions are essential institutions.

The biggest labour organisation is the Deutscher Gewerkschaftsbund, DGB for short (German Trade Union Federation), which has about eleven million members in sixteen unions.

The DGB recruits and represents members from specific industries rather than from specific occupations. Thus a secretary, a printer, an accountant and a delivery driver working in a printing factory could all belong to the IG Druck und Papier (the printing and paper workers' union).

Another big trade union organisation is the Deutsche Angestellten-Gewerkschaft, DAG for short, which is the union of salaried employees and has 578,000 members. The Deutscher Beamtenbund, DBB, is the civil servants' federation with about one million members. The Christlicher Gewerkschaftsbund CGB (Christian Trade Union Federation) with its affiliated unions has 316,000 members.

There is no closed shop system in Germany, and no one can be forced to join a union. The unions are not connected with a particular party or church, although the DGB is slightly more left-wing in its approach than, say, the CGB.

Most employers are organised in a branch of the Bundesvereinigung der Deutschen Arbeitgeberverbände, DBA for short (Confederation of German Employers' Associations). The trade unions and employers' organisations relevant to an industry or professional group negotiate collective agreements for work conditions and payment.

Membership in a trade union has several advantages:

- You can get advice about your work contract.

- You may be entitled to legal aid from your union in a dispute with your employers.

- The union provides you with information, such as collective agreements, which give you an idea how much you should get paid for your work.

- The unions maintain colleges and training centres for members; you may get free training in public speaking, negotiation skills and so on.

- Trade union activities can enrich your social life, especially when you are new to an area and don't know anybody.

Addresses of trade unions and professional associations

Deutscher Gewerkschaftsbund, Hans-Böckler-Str. 39, D-40476 Düsseldorf, Germany.

Deutsche Angestelltengewerkschaft, Karl-Muck-Platz 1, D-20355 Hamburg, Germany.

DJV-Hilfsverein (journalists' association), Regine Sakowsky, Bennauerstr. 60, D-53115 Bonn, Germany. Tel: (228) 222976. Fax: (0228 214917)

Christlicher Gewerkschaftsbund Deutschlands, Konstantinstr. 13, D-53179 Bonn, Germany.

Bundesvereinigung der Deutschen Arbeitgeberverbände, Gustav-Heinemann-Ufer 72, D-50968 Köln, Germany.

Bund Deutscher Sekretärinnen e.V. (Federation of German Secretaries), Zentnerstr. 44, D-90796 München, Germany. Tel: (089) 2716773. Fax: (089) 2724285.

Deutscher Journalistenverband (German Journalists Association), Bennauerstr. 60, D-53115 Bonn, Germany.

IG Medien, (Print Media Union), Friedrichstr. 15, D-70174 Stuttgart, Germany.

Journalisten helfen Journalisten e.V. (journalists' initiative), Christiane Schlötzer-Sootland, Frauenstr. 12, D-80469 München, Germany. Tel./Fax: (089) 223667.

Medien gegen Rassismus (journalists' movement against racism), Ralf Radler, Medienfabrik, Hans-Böckler-Str. 163, D-50354 Köln, Germany. Tel: (0221) 456-2753. Fax: (0221) 456-2795.

Verband Deutscher Drehbuchautoren (German script writers' association), Rosenthaler Str. 39, D-10178 Berlin, Germany. Tel: (030) 2824205. Fax: (030) 2823700.

Vereinigung Deutscher Reisejournalisten (German travel journalists' association), Gollenstr 25, D-73733 Esslingen, Germany. Tel: (0711) 378007. Fax: (0711) 378040.

HOURS OF WORK

The average working day begins at 8 a.m. and finishes at 5 p.m., with one hour for lunch, and Saturdays and Sundays free, and an early end on Fridays. The average working week is 35–40 hours.

HANDING IN YOUR NOTICE

German employment contracts usually say you must give notice six weeks before you plan to leave, and the last day must be the last day of the quarter, that is 31 March, 30 June, 30 September or 31 December. If you have a managerial job, your period of notice may be longer.

ANNUAL LEAVE

How much annual leave you get depends on your individual contract, which is usually based on a collective agreement between the employers and the trade unions. It can be anything between 24 and 44 days paid leave, although the statutory requirement is far less. Most get around 35 days.

HOW TO GET ON WITH COLLEAGUES

Germans are formal in their work relationships. Colleagues call one another 'Herr Müller' and 'Frau Maier' and 'Sie' instead of 'Klaus', 'Renate' and 'du'.

The dress code is slightly less formal than in Britain. For example, a secretary wears a blouse and skirt rather than a suit. Keep your office door closed. Your colleagues do the same. This is to save heating costs, to maintain privacy, and to avoid being disturbed at work.

Be punctual and reliable. German bosses value punctuality as an important virtue.

Einstand und Ausstand

In many trades it is customary that new workers and employees pay *Einstand*, to buy their colleagues' goodwill. For example, you can take them for drinks to the pub after the first working day, or bring a tray of cakes into the office.

Ask the colleague with whom you are working closely what is customary in the company, and follow his or her advice. It is acceptable to provide Einstand on the second or third day of work.

Similarly, a colleague who is leaving pays *Ausstand*. On your birthday, you are expected to bring cakes for the people with whom you are sharing an office. Observe the customs in your company and follow other colleagues' examples.

CASE STUDIES

Claire finds the work hard

'I had expected to meet a professional challenge, but secretarial work is the same all over the world. The real challenge lies in doing what I've been doing for years, in foreign surroundings, using a language which is not my native tongue. I find the Germans work hard and show great discipline, at least at the bank where I'm now. No prolonged tea breaks, no gossip in the ladies' room. Sometimes I long for a relaxing chat. But I have twice as much annual leave than I had in the UK, which compensates for it.'

Sarah: an older sister rather than an au pair

'My au pair family had two boys: Pirmin, who was just two years old, and Jonas who was six months. They seemed really nice and not a bit like what everyone in England had predicted. Naturally I got to know them really well. According to contract, my day-to-day duties were to look after the children for four hours a day, but neither the parents nor I wanted me to be a mechanical robot who switched off after duty hours. I became more like an older sister to the children than an au pair, and the arrangement suited me brilliantly. My job was to keep the children happy and to stop them from killing themselves or each other. But I had never met two brothers who loved each other so much as these two. I love them both as if they were my brothers and I would do anything for them.'

Kevin impresses the boss

'When my boss said ''You're almost as good as a German,'' he meant it as a compliment. He is pleased with my work. Like many German builders, he has recruited an international workforce, with people from Britain, France, Poland, Romania, Greece, Turkey and the former Yugoslavia.

'Brickies from Britain have a good reputation: on average, we have more skill and experience than those from other countries. We know what we are doing and therefore work better and faster. Our disadvantage, according to my boss, is that we are too lazy to learn the language. He is probably right. We have a weird situation here: eight nationalities, eight languages, yet we communicate with each other all the time, mostly by sign language.'

USEFUL WORDS AND PHRASES

Anstellungsvertrag   employment contract
Arbeitgeber   employer
Arbeitnehmer   employee
Arbeitsvertrag   work contract
Ausbildungsvertrag   training contract
Betriebsrat/Betriebsrätin   male/female shop steward
Dreizehntes Monatsgehalt   13th monthly salary
Fixum   basic fixed salary
Gehalt   salary
Gehaltserhöhung   salary increase
Gewerkschaft   trade union
Gleitzeit   flexitime
Kollege/Kollegin   male/female colleague
Kündigungsfrist   period of notice
Probezeit   trial period
Provision   commission
Tarifvertrag   collective agreement about working conditions between trade unions and employers
Teilzeit   part time
Überstunden   overtime
Urlaubsanspruch   annual leave entitlement

9
Living in Germany

SHOPPING IN GERMANY

People queue at supermarket check-outs, but not in shops which have a single long counter. There, you may have to fight your way forward until you attract the attention of the sales assistant. Be persistent and, if necessary, use your physical strength (except when there is a wheel-chair user, a frail old person or a parent with a pram).

Opening Hours

Shop opening hours are strictly regulated and can be inconvenient for full-time employees. Typical opening times in rural areas are Monday to Friday 8.00–12.00 and 14.30–18.00, Saturday 8.00–12.00. In urban areas, shops are likely to open Monday to Saturday 9.00–13.00 and 14.00–18.30. Department stores stay open during lunch-time.

Sunday trading is forbidden. There are a few exceptions, for example shops at railway stations which provide food for travellers. Furniture stores may open their display rooms for prospective clients on Sundays, but are not allowed to give advice or conclude sales.

Shops can get permission to keep their doors open until 20.30 on Thursdays. Some department stores, hairdressers and beauticians have taken the opportunity, but there is a strong resistance from the trade unions.

In some regions, shops don't trade on Wednesday afternoons. Most hairdressing salons stay closed on Mondays.

Sales

Germany has strict rules on price-slashing. There are only two seasonal sales, each lasting two weeks only: *Winterschlußverkauf* (at the end of January) and *Sommerschlußverkauf* (at the end of July).

At the department store

Many of the large department stores have a food department, which is usually on the basement level. A department store is called *Kaufhaus*.

Buying food

You buy your meat either at the butcher's *(Metzgerei or Schlachterei)*, or from large food stores. Special dairy and cheese shops (*Käserei* or *Meierei*) have become almost extinct, although some new shops have opened recently; you are more likely to buy your cheese at a general food store.

Germans like to buy their food often and get it fresh. Therefore, you can buy cold meats and cheese in quantities as small as 100 g. Say if you want them in slices *(in Scheiben)* or in a piece *(am Stück)*. Because of campaigns to avoid unnecessary waste, you may have to bring your own suitable, clean plastic container which will be filled and sealed at the counter.

For bread, you to go a *Bäckerei*. In Germany, you will find bread in amazing variety, including many wholegrain and healthy loaves. Jam-filled doughnuts are called *Berliner* (except in Berlin) – you can imagine that John F. Kennedy's famous statement '*Ich bin ein Berliner*' caused some hilarity. There's another sweet pastry, shaped like a mound and iced on the base, called *Amerikaner* (American), so don't say '*Ich bin ein Amerikaner*' when asked for your nationality.

Don't forget to eat *Brezeln* or *Pretzeln* (the spelling and the size both depend on the region), which go wonderfully with beer. Rolls are called *Brötchen*. A filled roll is called a *Sandwich* or *belegtes Brötchen*, and a sandwich is called *belegtes Brot*.

You can buy almost everything in Germany that you would find in UK shops, with the exception of Marmite and lemon curd, so take a supply if you can't live without them. You may not find parsnips, but a surprising variety of radishes which are rich in vitamins, keep well, and add a hot flavour to salads.

There are not many corner shops *(Tante-Emma-Läden)* in Germany.

Health and beauty

For health food, you go to a *Reformhaus*. Medicines (both prescription and non-prescription) are available from the *Apotheke*. You cannot buy painkillers at a grocer's shop, and you may find that Apotheke prices are steep.

Most medicines prescribed by a doctor are free, but you have to pay a small administration charge for each prescription. In addition to

Einkaufsliste *Shopping list*

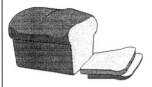

Brot	bread	Eier (von frei-	(freerange)
Weißbrot	*white bread*	**laufenden**	*eggs*
Schwarzbrot	*dark bread*	**Hühnern)**	
Vollkornbrot	*wholemealbread*	**Nudeln**	*noodles*
Brötchen	*bread roll*	**Reis**	*rice*
Kuchen	*cake*	**Öl**	*oil*
Torte	*gateau*	**Essig**	*vinegar*
Kekse	*biscuits*	**Fett**	*fat*
Mehl	*flour*	**Bonbons**	*sweets*

		Haferflocken	*oatflakes*
		Fertiggericht	*ready meal*
		Kaffee	*coffee*
		(löslich)	*(instant)*
		Tee	*tea*
		Teebeutel	*teabags*
Käse	*cheese*	**Kräutertee**	*herbal tea*
Joghurt	*yoghurt*	**Honig**	*honey*
Quark	*curd cheese*	**Marmelade**	*jam*
Milch	*milk*	**Getreideflocken**	*cereals*
Vollmilch	*full-cream*	**Hefe**	*yeast*
entrahmt	*skimmed*	**Waschmittel**	*detergent*
Butter	*butter*	**Spülmittel**	*washing-up*
Margarine	*margarine*		*liquid*
Hüttenkäse	*cottage cheese*	**Putzmittel**	*cleanser*

Fig. 7. Shopping list.

Einkaufsliste *Shopping list*

Obst	fruit
Gemüse	vegetables
Äpfel	apples
Birnen	pears
Pflaumen	plums
Trauben	grapes
Erdbeeren	strawberries
Orangen	oranges
Walnüsse	walnuts
Haselnüsse	hazelnuts
Bananen	bananas
Zitronen	lemons
Pilze	mushrooms
Paprika	peppers
Rotkohl	red cabbage
Weißkohl	white cabbage
Kopfsalat	lettuce
Spargel	asparagus
Gurken	cucumbers
Bohnen	beans
Erbsen	peas
Lauch	leeks
Tomaten	tomatoes
Kartoffeln	potatoes
Rüben	carrots

Fleisch	meat
Wurst	sausage
Geflügel	poultry
Fisch	fish
Meeresfrüchte	seafood
Rindfleisch	beef
Schweinefleisch	pork
Wild	game
Hackfleisch	minced meat

Getränke	drinks
Bier	beer
Rotwein	red wine
Weißwein	white wine
Apfelsaft	apple juice
Orangensaft	orange juice
Mineralwasser	mineral water
Limonade	lemonade

Fig. 7. Continued.

medicines, the Apotheke sells some general beauty and healthcare products.

A *Drogerie*, despite its name, does not sell drugs. it is similar to a Boots outlet, offering general healthcare products, cosmetics, perfumes, photo development, health food, some stationery and household items, personal hygiene products and baby food. Prices at a Drogerie tend to be lower than at an Apotheke.

Perfumes and cosmetics are also sold at the *Parfümerie*, but they stock only the classy, expensive brands.

You will look in vain for witchhazel in drugstores. This 'first aid' remedy, popular in the UK, is little known in Germany. You can buy it under the name *Hamamelis* in an Apotheke.

The Germans have their own versatile miracle remedy, the German Chamomile (*Kamille*). Buy dried flowers in the Apotheke, Drogerie or Reformhaus, put them into a saucepan with water, bring to the boil, take off the heat, brew for three minutes, then strain.

You can drink the infusion to calm the nerves, to sleep better, to bring relief in case of stomach disorders, diarrhoea, flu, cold, or any infectious disease. You can add it to your bath-water to soothe allergies and rashes, dab it on your spots to reduce acne, or rinse your hair with it to get a blonde shine.

Contraception

You can buy condoms in a Drogerie or in an Apotheke, and sometimes in other shops. Pessaries are available only in Apotheken.

For all other forms of contraception (IUD, pill and so on), you need a prescription which you get from a gynaecologist. There are several gynaecologists in each town.

The pill is free if it is prescribed for health reasons (PMS, acne, hirsutism), but you have to pay the full price if it is for contraception. You may find this confusing if you come from the UK where it is free as a contraceptive but must be paid for if it's for medical treatment. So if you need both a contraceptive and an acne remedy, make sure you give your acne as the main reason.

Buying by mail order

As in other countries, you can buy clothes, toys, furniture and household equipment from mail order catalogues. It is convenient getting items delivered to your doorstep and trying them on and out at home. But the hassle involved if something goes wrong, doesn't fit, or paperwork gets mixed up, can be a nuisance.

Addresses
Verandhaus Klingel, D-75160 Pforzheim, Germany.

Baur Versand, Bahnhofstr. 10, D-96222 Burgkunstadt, Germany.

Otto Versand, Bestellservice, D-20088 Hamburg, Germany.

Stiftung Warentest
This foundation calls itself 'the strong partner of the critical consumer'. It tests products and publishes the results. Test criteria can involve the longevity of an item, how user- and environment-friendly it is, and its safety. The tests are objective and many Germans prefer to buy products which did well in the tests. Stiftung Warentest publishes a magazine, *Test*, which is available by subscription. Each issue covers several product groups. If you plan to live in Germany for a long time and are going to buy household equipment and other items, the information published in the magazine is invaluable.

There is also a telephone information service which deals with some 75,000 consumer enquiries a year.

Address: Stiftung Warentest, Lützowplatz 11-13, D-10785 Berlin, Germany. Tel: (031) 2631-0. Information helpline: (03)0 2623014.

Arbeitsgemeinschaft der Verbraucherverbände
Another organisation which represents the consumers' interests is the *Arbeitsgemeinschaft der Verbraucherverbände* (AgV). This is the umbrella organisation of German consumer and socio-political groups. It supplies factual information on a wide range of topics: food, health, the environment, finance, homes, hobbies, leisure, household affairs, energy consumption and consumer rights. There is also a monthly magazine, *Verbraucher Rundschau*.

The AgV supplies brochures on subjects such as dealing with mould on walls, saving money on heating bills, making gardens safe for children, protecting children from drowning, funeral services, dating agencies, keeping dogs, repair service bills, and advice on buying furniture. Each brochure or booklet is published in German and costs between DM 1 and DM 15. For titles and prices contact the AgV. There is also a booklet in English, called *The Consumer Associations and Their Work*.

If you need advice, for example how to complain about faulty goods or dishonest services, you can contact the local *Verbraucher-Zentrale*. There is one in every city. You find the addresses in telephone directories or can get them from the AgV.

Address: Arbeitsgemeinschaft der Verbraucherverbände e.V., Heils-bachstr. 20, D-53123 Bonn, Germany. Tel: (0228) 6489-0. Fax: (0228) 644258.

MAKING FRIENDS

Making friends in Germany is easier than in the UK, because you are not offending against any society rule by talking to people to whom you have not been introduced.

Just ring at your neighbour's doorbell and introduce yourself. You may also talk to people in the commuter train, bus or underground. Just remember to stick to small talk at first, and let the others decide after a few sentences if they are interested in continuing the conversation.

Good places to meet people are universities and polytechnics; get their programme of events (dances, festivals, talks) and join in. You can also go to a pub; choose one which is frequented by people of the same age group.

Courses, groups and clubs

Adult education courses provide a good opportunity for meeting people who share your interests, and many Germans enrol for a course because they want to make new friends. It usually takes two or three evenings before someone suggests going to have a drink together. It is all right for you to take the initiative. Adult education centres are called *Volks-hochschule*.

You can join a group, society or club. Many clubs are organised in nationwide associations, such as the *Turn- und Sportverein* (sports club), the *Wanderverein* (the equivalent of the Ramblers' Association) or the *Deutscher Skatverband* (Skat Association, see below). Most of them welcome new members.

A fairly new type of group, which has appeared since the 1970s, is a *Bürgerinitiative* (citizens' initiative), a form of action group. A group of citizens get together, often spontaneously, to draw public attention to a problem which they feel has been neglected by the authorities, or to try to remedy a grievance. These can be small and local (perhaps to get a children's playground in the neighbourhood) or have hundreds of members (for example, with the aim of preventing the building of a new airport runway).

German law allows and encourages such assemblies and peaceful demonstrations, and although the groups have no power, they can be influential at the planning stage.

If you feel a bit daunted about joining a German group or club where you may be the only foreigner, especially if you don't speak the language yet, you can join a British-German (or your nationality-German) friendship club. You find them in most cities and many towns. They are listed in the telephone directories as 'Anglo-German Club' or 'Deutsch-Britische Gesellschaft'. Some addresses are listed in the Further Reading section at the end of this book.

PRACTISING YOUR HOBBIES

If cricket is your hobby, you may find it difficult to practise it in Germany. Football and tennis, on the other hand, are popular.

Writers may be disappointed that there are few writers' circles, and you have to be lucky to find an amateur dramatic society. However, there are many music clubs and bands.

Playing cards

Few people know how to play bridge. Popular German card-games include *Sechsundsechzig*, *Doppelkopf*, *Rommé*, *Mau-Mau* and *Skat*. The rules for Mau-Mau, which can be played in a large group with any number of players, differ from village to village, so make sure you agree on the rules before you start playing.

If you enjoy card-games, learn Skat. This game is played almost exclusively in Germany and in Canada. Its rules are complex, and regulated by the Deutscher Skatverband. The game may seem a little confusing at first, but if you have mastered bridge, you will find it easy. You don't need a huge stock of words, but you must be able to count to 200 in German.

The game needs three players. Often there are two people in a pub, in a canteen, on a beach or in a park who are looking for a third person, so it is a good method of making friends. You can also join a local Skat club. There are more men than women among the members, but the Deutscher Skatverband actively encourages women to join. You usually play for nominal amounts of money, and there are also competitions.

Of the 32 cards, each player receives ten. The other two are put aside and called the Skat. The players bid against one another. They calculate their maximum bids by the value of what they wish to be trump, and by the number of knaves they hold.

The one who bids highest may choose what is trump in this game: clubs (*Kreuz*), spades (*Pik* or *Schippe*), hearts (*Herz*) or diamonds (*Karo*). Alternatively, the bidder plays a grand, in which the knaves

(*Buben*) alone are trump cards. There is also a *Null* (zero), where the players try to get as many points as possible. The player also picks up the Skat and puts away two other cards of his or her choice.

The two lower bidders become allies, and their points are added up. If they achieve more points than the player, the player has lost the game. In a Null game, the player loses if the allied opponents can force him or her to take a trick.

COOKING AND BAKING

German cookers and cooking utensils are the same as in the UK, but your oven may not have a grill. You may find it more difficult to buy fresh mushrooms, and it is almost impossible to find potatoes large enough to make decent jacket potatoes.

In rural areas, you may be expected to serve your tea guests coffee (made with a proper coffee-maker) and a home-made cake. When buying a book with bakery recipes, take care to select one which explains the dough-making step by step, not just 'prepare so-and-so dough', because German cakes and gateaux are based on different dough recipes.

Flädlessuppe (pancake soup)

This is a popular dish made with leftover pancakes, served as a starter or as a snack meal.

Prepare a clear soup, using stock cubes and water. Cut pancakes into long thin strips. This is easiest if you roll them up and cut the rolls. Add the strips to the simmering soup, remove from the heat and serve when the strips are soft, but before they start disintegrating. Garnish with fresh herbs, for example chopped chives.

If you don't have leftover pancakes, you can make them using 25 g flour, 1 egg, 75 ml semi-skimmed milk and a little salt. Leave the dough to stand for a few minutes before making pancakes.

Pellkartoffeln

This is the German equivalent to baked potatoes. For each person, you need 250 g medium-sized potatoes.

Wash and brush the potatoes, but do not peel. Boil or steam the potatoes until soft (check by piercing them with a fork).

Serve them hot in their skins. Serve about 100 g Quark (curd cheese) per person. Even better, use Kräuterquark, by adding fresh chopped herbs to the Quark. In some regions, a slice of cheese is served as well.

Eat the potatoes without the skins: spear them with your fork in your left hand, and peel them with the knife in your right. Cut them in slices and eat them with a touch of butter.

Semmelknödel (bread dumplings)

Dumplings are immensely popular in Germany, and usually accompany meat dishes. They may be boiled, poached, fried or baked. This recipe is economical and easy to prepare.

8 stale bread rolls	300 ml milk
half an onion (finely chopped)	2 eggs
parsley (finely chopped)	60 g flour
salt	1 teaspoon baking powder
50 g butter	

Quarter the bread rolls, and fry them with onion, parsley and salt in butter until golden brown. Place in a mixing bowl, cover with boiling milk and let this soak in. Add eggs, flour and baking powder, and work the whole into a soft dough. Shape fairly large dumplings and simmer them gently in salted water for 10 minutes.

Spätzle

Spätzle is an everyday pasta dish from Schwaben (Swabia) where it is eaten with almost any savoury dish. These little noodles are considered to be genuine only if made by hand.

450 g flour	enough liquid (half water, half milk) to form a very soft dough
3 eggs	
$^1/_2$ teaspoon salt	1 tablespoon butter for garnish

Sift flour, make a well in the middle and pour in eggs, beaten up with the salt. Starting from the middle, mix eggs into flour, gradually adding liquid until you get a very soft dough. Beat and knead the dough until it forms blisters. Place it on to a chopping board and scrape thin strips of dough straight into boiling, salted water with the broad side of a knife. Let them swell up for 3 minutes, fish them out with a sieve, rinse in hot water and place them in a serving bowl. Repeat until all the dough has been used up. Before serving, toss the Spätzle in browned butter.

Nürnberger Lebkuchen

Nürnberg, noted for its heritage of art and architecture, is also famous for its Christmas market and gingerbread. This recipe from the Middle Ages received its name *Lebkuchen* (cake of life) from the natural ingredients and spices it uses, which were considered to possess life-sustaining and stimulating qualities. At Christmas, a gingerbread house is a firm favourite with young and old.

350 g honey	$^1/_2$ teaspoon ground cloves
150 g caster sugar	$^1/_2$ teaspoon ground cinnamon
750 g flour	$^1/_2$ teaspoon ground ginger
1 pinch baking soda	150 g mixed peal
1 teaspoon baking powder	sugar glaze
250 g chopped almonds	

Bring the honey, with half the sugar, to boiling point, and keep boiling until it drops in beads from the spoon. Leave to cool, then pour it over the sieved flour. Add the baking powder and baking soda. Knead to a smooth dough and leave for two days in a cool place. Boil the remaining sugar with a little water to a syrup. Quickly sauté the almonds in this. Blend the syrup and almonds into the dough as quickly as possible, adding the spices. Roll out the dough (about 1 cm thick) on a floured board. Cut into biscuit-sized oblongs with a sharp knife, sprinkle with the chopped peel and leave in a warm place for a day. Finally bake in a hot oven, at 220 degrees Celsius, for 25 minutes. Remove from the oven and while still warm brush with a sugar glaze.

Schwarzwälder Kirschtorte (Black Forest gateau)

Getting this gateau just right requires skill and experience. Not for beginners!

110 g butter	50 g cornflour
100 g sugar	2 teaspoons baking powder
1 packet vanilla sugar	7 tablespoons kirsch
4 eggs	$^1/_2$ litre cream
70 g grated almonds	750 g sour cherries (from a jar)
100 g grated plain chocolate	1 tablespoon chocolate flakes
50 g flour	extra butter for the baking tin

Grease a springform tin (26 cm diameter) with butter. Pre-heat the oven to 180 degrees Celsius. Beat butter, sugar and vanilla sugar until frothy, gradually adding eggs, almonds and chocolate. Mix flour, cornflour and baking powder and fold in. Place dough in springform tin and bake in the bottom half of the oven for 30–40 minutes. Stand to cool. Wait for at least two hours. Cut twice horizontally. Put drops of kirsch on the base. Whip cream with a little sugar until stiff. Drain the cherries. Spread the cream 2 cm high on the base and on the first layer of the cake. Spread the cherries on both.

Then spread cream only on the top layer, and sprinkle the centre with chocolate flakes. Pile the layers on top of each other. Use the remaining cream to pipe rosettes on the top of the gateau and decorate each with a cherry.

Apfelmus (apple purée)

For this delicious dessert you can use windfalls. There is no need to peel them. Add cinnamon and cloves for a spicier version.

1 kg apples
150 ml water
3 heaped tablespoons sugar

Cut the apples into small wedges, add the water and simmer gently until the fruit is soft. Rub through a sieve and add sugar to taste. If you like, add a handful of stoned raisins and chopped almonds. Place the purée in a glass bowl and serve as a dessert or as an accompaniment to potato cakes or waffles.

GOING OUT

Fast food

You won't find fish and chips or jacket potatoes. Hamburgers (called hamburgers) are available at MacDonalds and other American-style outlets. Chips are called *Pommes Frittes* or *Fritten*, and crisps are called *chips*.

Additional confusion may be caused by 'hot' which is *heiss* if it refers to temperature and *scharf* if it refers to flavour. *Scharf* also means sharp in the sense of knife-like but not in the sense of sharp-flavoured, for which the Germans say *sauer*.

Typical German fast food includes:

- Bratwurst (friend sausage).

- Red or white Grillwurst (also a fried sausage).

- Fleischkäse (a slice of meat loaf, usually squeezed between two halves of a bread roll, with plenty of mustard).

- Currywurst (sliced fried sausage in plenty of hot tomato ketchup and curry powder, eaten with a toothpick).

- Brathähnchen (chicken).

Going for drinks

German pubs are called *Kneipen*. The singular is *Kneipe*. You can get a variety of beers, as well as some wines and soft drinks. Every Kneipe has a *Stammtisch*, a table reserved for regular customers who always come on the same day at the same time, often to play Skat.

There are also plenty of *Bierstuben* (beer pubs) and *Weinstuben* (wine bars) some of which serve meals as well. If they have a garden attached, they may be called a *Biergarten* or a *Weingarten*.

The regulations for opening hours are complex and depend on local circumstances, but most pubs are open until long after midnight.

It's all right to go to a pub alone, even if you haven't been there before. But you may feel more comfortable choosing one where you have been previously with other people. It's also a good idea to patronise a particular pub or two regularly, so the staff there get to know you and make you feel welcome.

The German terms for 'cheers' are *prost, prosit,* or *zum Wohl.*

Wine

Most Germans like their wine to be *trocken* (dry), especially when drinking it with a meal. Liebfraumilch, which is so well-known abroad, is drunk mostly as an accompaniment to sweets or cakes. Sweet wine is called *süß* or sometimes *naß* (wet).

Germany has so many different wine varieties, quality categories and regulations that you would need years to study them. *Tafelwein* is table wine, which is the right bottle to take on a picnic but not to give as a gift. *Qualitätswein* is of a higher quality, the sort you can serve to your guests or take to a party. *Qualitätswein mit Prädikat* is top quality, and makes a welcome gift. *Spätlese* (late harvest) is sweet, expensive, and served on special occasions with a dessert. *Eiswein* (ice wine) is from grapes picked in December after a frost, expensive, and given as a special gift or served instead of a dessert.

You will gain goodwill if you order locally produced varieties.

Beer
Beer varieties are plentiful. It is estimated that about 1,000 breweries produce 4,000 varieties of beer. They brew according to the German *Reinheitsgebot*, a purity law which dates from the sixteenth century and stipulates that only hops, malt, yeast and water can be used. The Germans are proud of their beers and regard foreign beer as 'impure', although EU legislation has forced them to let foreign brands into their country.

Try the local varieties. You can order a small beer (*'Ein kleines Bier, bitte'*) or a large beer (*'Ein großes Bier, bitte'*). How large a small or a large beer is depends on the region. In Bavaria, where they drink beer in litre glasses, a small beer may be larger than a large one in another Bundesland.

Restaurants
A restaurant is called *Restaurant*, sometimes pronounced the French way. An inn is called *Gaststube*, *Gasthaus* or *Gastwirtschaft*. If you want one with German cuisine, watch out for the words *'gutbürgerliche Küche'* which can be translated literally as 'good citizens' kitchen'.

There are few Chinese and Indian restaurants, but plenty of places run by Italian, Greek and Turkish nationals who provide their cuisine.

In most restaurants, you can choose your own table. You may choose to share a table with someone already sitting there. In this case you say *'Ist dieser Platz frei?'* (is this seat vacant) or *'Sind diese Plätze frei?'* (are these seats vacant). When the reply contains the word *'belegt'* (occupied), you can't sit down. When someone just starts eating, say *'Guten Appetit'* (have a good appetite).

Popular dishes in Germany include:

● Sauerbraten (braised beef marinated in vinegar).

● Sauerkraut (pickled cabbage).

● Spätzle (Swabian pasta).

● Maultaschen (pasta squares filled with spinach and served in a clear soup).

● Blut- und Leberwurst (sausage-shaped hides each filled with hot, almost liquid paste, one made with blood, one with liver, usually served with Sauerkraut and mashed potato).

VORSPEISEN	STARTERS
Kartoffelsuppe	*potato soup*
Zwiebelsuppe	*onion soup*
Tomatensuppe	*tomato soup*
Gemischter Salat	*mixed salad*

HAUPTGERICHTE	MAIN DISHES
Fischfilet	*fish fillet*
Schweinebraten	*pot-roast pork*
Rinderbraten	*pot-roast beef*
Spaghetti mit Tomatensauce	*Spaghetti with tomato sauce*
Auflauf	*pie, baked pudding*
Gemüseeintopf	*vegetable stew*

BEILAGEN	SIDE DISHES
Reis	*rice*
Gemüse	*vegetables*
Nudeln	*noodles*
Spätzle	*Swabian pasta*
Pommes frites	*chips*
Kartoffenbrei	*mashed potato*

Fig. 8. Looking at a German menu.

NACHSPEISEN	DESSERTS
Eis mit Sahne	Icecream with cream
Obstsalat	fruit salad
Apfelkuchen	apple cake
Schwarzwälder Kirschtorte	Black Forest gateau

HEISSE GETRÄNKE	HOT DRINKS
Kaffee	Coffee
Schwarztee	Tea
Kräutertee	herbal tea
Kakao	cocoa
(Tasse/Kännchen)	(cup/pot)

KALTE GETRÄNKE	COLD DRINKS
Rotwein	red wine
Weißwein	white wine
(trocken/süß)	(dry/sweet)
Bier	beer
(alkoholarm)	(low alcohol)
Mineralwasser	mineral water
Apfelsaft	apple juice
Orangensaft	orange juice
Limonade	lemonade
(Glas /Flasche)	(glass/bottle)

Fig. 8. Continued.

- Berliner Leber (liver, Berlin-style), Knödel (huge dumplings).

- Handkäs mit Musik (transparent cheese served with vinaigrette).

- Frankfurter Kranz (ring-shaped gateau, rich, filled with cream, irresistible in taste but high in calories).

Germans harvest asparagus when it is white, with pink tips. They may be horrified at the thought of eating it when it has tuned green. Try the white asparagus with savoury pancakes, thin slices of boiled ham and a white sauce.

Portions tend to be large and the quality excellent. Vegetarians may be disappointed. In a large city you may find a vegetarian restaurant, but ordinary restaurants don't have vegetarian menus or dishes. The chef may take it as a personal affront if you refuse to eat the meat, and even if you convince them that you want vegetables only, they'll probably arrive in meat gravy.

VISITING SOMEONE'S HOME

When you are invited to someone's home, take a bunch of flowers and present them to the hostess. Alternatively, you may take a small gift for the child or the children: a bar of chocolate, postcards from your home country, a small picture book, some fruit, or a packet of coloured pencils.

If the occasion is a birthday, you can take either flowers or a gift. Consider something typical of your home country: a coffee-table book with pictures of English cottages or Scottish landscapes, a jar of lemon curd (unknown in Germany), Irish Whiskey, Californian wine. Small children love toy models of red London double-decker buses; teenagers who study English at school or college cherish British or American pop music magazines.

Remember to take some suitable gifts with you when you go to Germany.

ENTERTAINING AT HOME

Typical visiting time is 3 p.m. on a Sunday afternoon. Serve coffee (made with freshly ground coffee and a coffee-maker rather than instant) and cakes (if possible home-made).

Visitors are likely to bring flowers, so have vases in several sizes ready.

LOOKING AT CUSTOMS, TRADITIONS AND HOLIDAYS

The main festivals in Germany are Christmas and Carnival. In addition, there are plenty of regional and local events. You may miss St Valentine's Day which is little known, although the flower and chocolate industries do their best to promote it.

Halloween and Guy Fawkes Day are unknown, too, but some villages have a bonfire night with plenty of *Glühwein* (spiced wine) during Lent.

Christmas

The Germans take Christmas (*Weihnachten*) slightly more seriously than the British. Nobody would put up paper garlands or wear a funny hat. The Germans don't need to – they have plenty of opportunities for being silly during their carnival.

Christmas is a family event as in other countries. Every family has a Christmas tree. They sing carols and may go to midnight mass. They decorate the living-room with plenty of candles and fir branches, but they don't know holly and mistletoe.

Most Germans have an *Adventskranz*, which is a fir wreath with four candles. On the first Sunday of advent, one candle is lit; on the second Sunday, two candles, and so on.

Christmas cakes, Christmas puddings and mince pies are unknown. Instead, they have varieties of gingerbread, *Früchtebrot* and *Christstollen* (both types of fruit bread, the former dark, the latter light in colour).

In many regions it is customary for the housewife to bake at least one variety of Christmas biscuits, often according to a recipe handed down by generations. She then gives small bags or tins of her biscuits to all the neighbours, friends and relatives she visits, and in turn receives theirs. This way, one can get a huge variety. *Zitronenherzen* (lemon hearts), *Kokosmakronen* (coconut macaroons) and *Zimtsterne* (cinnamon stars) are popular. If you want to follow the custom, try the recipe for Nürnberger Lebkuchen on page 105.

Alternatively, you may want to introduce your German friends to mince pies.

Christmas cards are sent only to those relatives whom you don't see personally at Christmas. You don't have to give cards to all your neighbours and colleagues.

The great day for children is 24 December, because they get their presents on Christmas Eve. These are not delivered by Santa Claus, but by the Christ child.

Santa Claus comes on 6 December (in some regions on 5 December), carrying a sack full of nuts, apples and oranges. He is called either *Weihnachtsmann* and looks like Santa Claus, or St Nikolaus in which case he is dressed and behaves like a dignified sainted bishop. Sometimes he is accompanied by a servant called Ruprecht, dressed in dark furs, who carries the sack and who punishes the naughty children.

Epiphany

Children go from house to house in the evening, dressed up as the three wise men or kings. One of them has their face painted black and carries the star of Bethlehem. They sing a carol or recite a poem, and you give them some sweets or your spare Pfennige.

Carnival

German Carnival, called *Karneval* (eighteenth-century origins) or *Fasnacht* (pagan and medieval origins), begins on 11 November at 11.11 a.m., is interrupted for Christmas and continues until the beginning of Lent.

The climax is the last week, which is celebrated with many pageants and balls. The pubs are crammed full. Every town quarter or village has its own traditional costumes, often made from rags or with individually handcarved wooden masks. There are cabaret evenings during which the speakers make fun of local politics and events, often with a serious underlying message. On *Schmotziger Dunschtig* ('Greasy Thursday') and *Rosenmontag* (Rose Monday, usually seven weeks before Easter Monday) people may even wear fancy dress at work.

Schmotziger Dunschtig customs include eating jam doughnuts and attending balls wearing a white nightgown. Musicians with self-made instruments tour the pubs and get a free drink for each performance. Students get up early in the morning (sometimes at 3 a.m.) to wake up their teachers who must provide them with snacks and drinks. On the last day of Fasnacht, people meet in the local inns to eat snails.

Corpus Christi Day

Fronleichnam is celebrated only in Bundesländer, and has its own colourful customs, which include the creating of huge picture carpets made from blossoms in front of the church, and processions.

May Festival

The first of May is celebrated in a variety of ways. It's workers' day as well as the day for ramblers and hikers. Weather permitting, everyone goes on a hike or bicycling tour, and attaches a small twig of fresh green beech to the rucksuck or bicycle.

There is also a Maypole in the village, and there may be some dancing around it. Young men may put up a branch of beech outside their secret love's window or door.

Beer, wine and cider festivals

The high season for local festivals is autumn, when the first new wine arrives. Many towns other than München (Munich) have their Bierfest. Indeed, most town quarters have a Bierfest, a Weinfest, a Dorffest (village fair) and maybe a few other local festivals. Brush up on your waltzes and polkas, as they are the most popular dances.

GERMAN NEWSPAPERS AND MAGAZINES

Reading newspapers and magazines is an effective way of finding out what's going on in your neighbourhood and in your field of work or leisure interest. It is a useful occupation, too, if you want to pick up grammar and up-to-date terminology. You may want to take out a magazine subscription before you go to Germany, or on arrival.

You should subscribe to a regional daily newspaper. These papers carry national and international news on the first pages, and regional and local news inside. This way, you get all the essential news in a single publication. Newspapers and magazines are available from grocers' shops, stationery shops, and the small stalls which sell snack foods, ice cream and papers, called *Zeitungskiosk*.

Thousands of newspapers and magazines are published in Germany. Here is a selection.

Bunte: weekly magazine, targeted mainly at women. Mostly features about VIPs – politicians, industrialists, artists, miracle doctors – their loves and lives, successes and failures. Also news about motoring and

PUBLIC HOLIDAYS

	1995	1996	1997
Neujahr New Year's Day	01.01.	01.01.	01.01
Dreikönig* Epiphany	06.01.	06.01.	06.01.
Rosenmontag** Rose Monday	27.02.	19.02.	10.02.
Ostermontag Easter Monday	17.04.	08.04.	31.03.
Tag der Arbeit Labour Day	01.05.	01.05.	01.05.
Christi Himmelfahrt Ascension Day	25.05.	16.05.	08.05.
Pfingstmontag Whit Monday	05.06.	27.05.	19.05.
Fronleichnam*** Corpus Christi Day	15.06.	06.06.	29.05.
Mariä Himmelfahrt**** Ascension of the Virgin Mary	15.08.	15.08.	15.08.
Tag der Deutschen Einheit Day of Unity	03.10.	03.10.	03.10.
Reformationstag***** Day of Reformation	31.10.	31.10.	31.10.
Allerheiligen****** All Saints Day	01.11.	01.11.	01.11.
Buss- und Bettag Day of Prayer and Repentance	22.11.	22.11.	22.11.
Weihnachten Christmas	25./26.12.	25./26.12.	25./26.12.

*	In Baden-Württemberg and Bavaria
**	Not an official public holiday, but kept in many areas.
***	In Baden-Württemberg, Bayern, Hessen, Nordrhein-Westfalen, Rheinland-Pfalz, Saarland.
****	Saarland and Catholic areas of Bayern.
*****	Brandenburg, Mecklenburg-Westpommern, Sachsen, Sachsen-Anhalt, Thüringen.
******	in Baden-Württemberg, Bayern, Hessen, Nordrhein-Westfalen, Rheinland-Pfalz, Saarland and Catholic areas of Thüringen.

travel, financial and health advice. Has the image of a 'clean' magazine, suitable for family reading. Single issue: DM 4. Annual subscription: DM 204 (plus postage if outside Germany). Publisher: Burda, Arabella-str. 23, D-81925 München, Germany.

Elle: Monthly magazine, targeted at women in the 20-49 age group. Emphasis on fashion and beauty, also cars, travel, home furnishing. Publisher: Elle Verlag GmbH, Arabellastr. 23, D-81925 München, Germany.

Meine Familie & ich: Monthly magazine. Emphasis on cookery, with plenty of German and international recipes. Each issue dedicated to a particular subject. Single issue: DM 4.90. Sold exclusively in supermarkets and grocery stores. Publisher: Burda/Magazin Verlag, Arabellastr. 23, D-81925 München, Germany.

Carina: Monthly magazine for young creative women. Emphasis on fashion and sewing patterns, plus beauty, home furnishing and decorating, cooking. Some love, career, travel, health and environmental advice. Single issue: DM 4.50. Annual subscription rates on request. Burda, Arabellastr. 23, D-81925 München, Germany.

Marketing Journal: Bi-monthly magazine. Targeted at senior staff and top managers in marketing, sales and communications. Features cover publicity strategies, the effectiveness of advertisement designs and so on. Available only by subscription: DM 98.60 a year. Publisher: Marketing Journal Verlag, Koopstr. 20-22, D-20144 Hamburg, Germany.

!forbes: Monthly business magazine. Aimed mostly at men. Covers subjects such as tax advice and business horoscopes. Single issue: DM 7.50 (Germany), DM 8.20 + DM 3.00 for postage and packing (Europe including Great Britain), annual subscription DM 77.40 (plus postage if outside Germany). Address: Focus Magazin Verlag, Postfach 81 01 64, D-81901 München, Germany.

Focus: Weekly magazine with news articles and news features, around 200 pages per issue. Single issue DM 4, subscription prices on request. Address: Focus-Abonnentenservice, Postfach 1295, D-77649 Offenburg, Germany.

Fig. 9. German magazines.

Druck und Papier: Monthly newspaper for people working in the printing, publishing and pulp and paper industries. 16 pages. Annual subscription: DM 30. Subscription address: Verlagsanstalt W.E. Weinmann, Postfach 4160, D-70779 Filderstadt, Germany.

M Menschen – Machen – Medien: Monthly magazine (eleven issues per year), for people working in journalism, radio, film production and television. News, features, diary dates, advice. 48 A4 pages. Annual subscription DM 70. Subscription address: Verlagsanstalt W.E. Weinmann, Postfach 4160, D-70779 Filderstadt, Germany.

Kunst & Kultur: Magazine for people working in the fields of literature, performing arts, visual arts and music. News, features, advice. Nine issues per year. 48 A4 pages. Annual subscription: DM 50. Subscription address: Verlagsanstalt W.E. Weinmann, Postfach 4160, D-70779 Filderstadt, Germany.

Das Haus: Monthly. Europe's biggest home building and furnishing magazine. Plenty of suggestions for converting, extending, modernising, decorating and furnishing your place, complete with addresses and price examples. Single issue DM 2.40. Subscription: DM 20.50 (ten issues), plus postage if outside Germany. Publisher: Burda GmbH, Postfach 810164, D-81901 München.

Sekretariat: Monthly magazine for secretaries and personal assistants. About 70 A4 pages, illustrated in colour throughout. Plenty of features and news articles covering career advice, developments in office equipment and furniture, shorthand exercises, office administration, organising conferences and events, effective telephone techniques, how to liaise with managers, staff and customers. Subscription: DM 136.00 a year, plus postage if outside Germany. Publisher: Gabler Verlag, Taunusstr. 54, D-65183 Wiesbaden, Germany. Tel: (0611) 5340. Fax: (0611) 534400.

CASE STUDIES

Claire makes friends

'I made some friends at the local *Krabbelgruppe*, as they call a mother and toddler group. I've learnt to use local festivals – especially the carnival – for networking. That's how I finally found a flat, for example.'

Sarah enjoys the food

'The German food is lovely. I put on half a stone during my stay. The father of my au pair family was a cordon bleu cook. Bratwurst was my favourite food, but I couldn't bring myself to eat Sauerkraut.

'A lot of life in Germany happens in and around clubs. They are good for social life. Music clubs are important, and so is, of course, the TSV (*Turn- und Sportverein*/sports club).

'In my spare time I joined the music school which plays an important role in the life of many people from Heusenstamm. I play the trumpet so I could join a local band, and through them I met many people and made friends.'

Kevin enjoys the pub

'My social life revolves mostly around the local pub, where we meet every Friday evening and sometimes on other days as well. I've been to a disco occasionally, but I feel a little self-conscious there. In the pub it's easier. The man behind the bar there greets me each time with '*Hallo Kevin, wie geht's?*' so I feel comfortable there even when I'm on my own.

'I don't have as much contact with my neighbours or other people in the town as I would like to. That's mostly because I still don't speak much German, and here in the eastern part of Germany few people speak English.'

USEFUL WORDS AND PHRASES

am Stück   in a piece
Apotheke   pharmacy, chemist
Bäckerei   bakery
Briefmarke   postage stamp
Buchhandlung   bookshop
Drogerie   drugstore
Einschreiben   registered mail
Gasthof, Gasthaus   inn
Guten Appetit   have a good appetite, enjoy your meal
in Scheiben   in slices
Kaufhaus   department store
Kneipe   pub
Lebensmittelhandlung   grocer's
Metzgerei   butcher's
Ostern   Easter

Parfümerie   shop for fragrances and cosmetics
Postamt   post office
Postkarte   postcard
Prost, Prosit   cheers
Reformhaus   health food shop
Schlachterei   butcher's
Schreibwarengeschäft   stationery shop
Sommerschlußverkauf   end of summer season sale
Versandhandel   mail order trade
Volkshochschule   adult education centre
Vollkornbrot   wholegrain bread
Weihnachten   Christmas
Winterschlußverkauf   end of winter season sale
Wurst   sausage or cold meat
Zeitung   newspaper
Zeitschrift   magazine
Zeitungskiosk   news-stand
Zum Wohl   cheers

10
Education and Training

Education policies are the responsibility of the Bundesländer (see page 17). The state has only limited legislative and financial powers. It may participate in educational planning.

To aid the freedom of movement and free choice of career anywhere in Germany – as guaranteed by the Grundgesetz – the Bundesländer co-operate with each other, so that the structure of education is similar throughout Germany.

FINDING THE RIGHT SCHOOL FOR YOUR CHILD

The whole of the school system is subject to state supervision in Germany. As a rule, schools are state or local government establishments. Private schools are also subject to state control.

In the past, only primary and elementary schools were free. Pupils attending secondary schools had to pay school fees, which few parents could afford. This meant that, for a long time, the type of school a child attended depended on the material situation of the parents.

Now all state schools are free for all children.

Compulsory education

Compulsory education *(Schulpflicht)* begins on reaching the age of six in Germany.

As a general rule, full-time compulsory school attendance ends after a period of nine years. In some Bundesländer it is ten years.

Pupils who have completed these nine or ten years of full-time school and leave school are normally obliged to attend a vocational school **(Berufsschule)** for one day per week until their eighteenth birthday.

Kindergarten and primary school

Kindergarten places may be limited, and parents have to pay a fee.

Some of them are run by religious communities, and children belonging to these communities may be given preference.

There is a primary school *(Grundschule)* in almost every village. Children attend primary school for four years. At the end of the fourth year, parents and teachers assess the children's academic capacities and decide whether they should go on to elementary or higher secondary school. Admission depends on the marks achieved in the school report and/or an entrance examination.

Some parents feel that the age of ten is too early for such a decision. However, the decision is not irrevocable. For example, it is always possible to change to a less demanding level of education, and a pupil who has completed the elementary school can continue his or her studies at a secondary school afterwards.

Hauptschule

The Hauptschule is compulsory for all those pupils who, on completion of the Grundschule, do not go on to a higher secondary school. The Hauptschule finishes with Class 9 in some Bundesländer and Class 10 in others.

The following subjects are compulsory: German, one foreign language (usually English), mathematics, physics/chemistry, biology, geography, vocational studies, arts, music, religious instruction and physical education. As you can see, the curriculum is comprehensive, and provides your child with a sound basis in academic subjects, while the focus is on vocational skills. The number of weekly lessons is between 30 and 33.

Realschule

This higher secondary school takes students from Class 5 to Class 10. It prepares its pupils for careers which call for independence, responsibility and leadership in various vocational areas. The curriculum is similar to that of a Hauptschule, but subjects are tackled more intensively. There are several academic and creative optional courses, and the optional study of a second foreign language (usually French) is encourage. The number of weekly lessons is between 30 and 34. The school-leaving certificate is obtained after sitting for a final examination and is called *Mittlere Reife*.

Students take the Mittlere Reife certificate at the age of sixteen. The education they have gained at a Realschule is similar to an A level education in the UK. However, a Realschule education is broader than A level education, because students have to take more subjects (thirteen or more), but study them in less depth.

Gymnasium

A Gymnasium is the equivalent of a grammar school. It is attended by pupils from Class 5 to Class 13, and provides a wide general education with focus on academic subjects. A first (usually English) and a second (usually French) foreign language are obligatory.

There is also the option of a *Berufliches Gymnasium* (vocational college) which covers Class 11 to Class 13. Only students who have completed Class 10 at either a Realschule or a Gymnasium may attend a Berufliches Gymnasium. These vocational colleges provide a wide general education, but with focus on vocational skills. There is, for example, a *Hauswirtschaftliches Gymnasium* (where the main subject studied is household economics), a *Technisches Gymnasium* (main subject: technology) and a *Wirtschaftsgymnasium* (main subjects: economics and business studies).

During the last two years at a Gymnasium, students have a choice of main subjects and subsidiary subjects, but an astonishing number of courses are obligatory to ensure wide general knowledge.

The *Reifezeugnis* or *Abitur* is the certificate gained after completion of the Gymnasium. It is either a full *(Allgemeine Hochschulreife)* or a limited *(fachgebundene Hochschulreife)* certificate. Limited certificates are gained at vocational colleges. Full certificates are awarded to students of the general Gymnasium, as well as students at the vocational colleges who take a certain combination of courses and examinations, usually including French.

Most students are between 19 and 21 when they finish their Gymnasium education – the age at which they would have their university BA degree in their pocket in other countries. This is because they have to study so many subjects – nine or more – to gain the Abitur certificate.

The full certificate satisfies the entry requirements to any university (but this does not mean a guaranteed place). With a limited certificate, students may not be permitted to all university courses.

Gesamtschulen

Gesamtschulen combine several or all of the above-mentioned types of school, which makes it easier to switch from one level of achievement to the other without uprooting a child too much.

Vocational colleges

In addition to the Berufsbildende Gymnasium mentioned above, there are colleges which offer one- or two-year courses for graduates from a

Volksschule or a Realschule in technical or secretarial skills. These colleges are known by a variety of names, including *Berufsfachschule* or *Fachschule*. Most are state schools, but there are some private colleges, too (see page 128).

Private schools

German basic law guarantees the right to set up private schools. Currently, there are almost 3,000 private schools in Germany, including many boarding schools. Many are run by the Catholic and Protestant churches. The number of pupils attending private schools is somewhere over half a million.

Unlike in the UK, pupils who attend a private school do not automatically gain social or career advantages. Germans are not keen to send their children to a private school, even if they could afford it. This is partly because most parents are satisfied with the education provided by state schools.

The second reason is that there is a social stigma attached to private boarding schools. Children at boarding schools are regarded as poor little mites deserted by their indifferent parents.

The European School

The European School, based in Munich, provides school education from Grundschule Class 1 to Gymnasium Class 13, and finishes with an internationally recognised Abitur examination.

Pupils are educated in their mother tongue (for example, English), and study a foreign language (usually German) from their first year at primary school. A third language is compulsory from Class 7, and a fourth language is optional. Pupils gain a wide education, but the emphasis is on languages.

The European School is meant for children of the employees of EU institutions. Other children can be admitted if there are vacant places, and children of EU nationals and foreign diplomats are given priority. Pupils who join an advanced class need to have knowledge of one or more foreign language.

The annual fee for children whose parents are not employed by EU institutions is DM 1,876 for the Grundschule and DM 2,551 for the higher secondary school.

Address: Europäische Schule München, Elise-Aulinger-Str. 21, D-81739 München, Germany. Tel: (089) 6372611. Fax: (089) 6378418.

Foreign pupils in the German school system

In the 1989/90 school year, prior to unification, 930,400 foreign pupils were attending normal schools, vocational schools and colleges in the Federal Republic of Germany.

At 10.3 per cent, the proportion of foreign pupils in the overall pupil population achieved a new high in 1989. By way of comparison, the number of foreign pupils came to no more than 1.7 per cent in 1970.

The majority of foreign pupils come from the six countries of origin of guest workers in the FRG: Greece, Italy, Portugal, Spain, Turkey and Yugoslavia.

Additional coaching

Foreign pupils and students have the same rights and duties as their German classmates. Mastery of the German language is the major requirement to ensure that children obtain final academic and vocational qualifications. As long as they have the required knowledge of German they are put into normal classes according to their age and achievement level.

At the same time, it is important to foster their native culture and mother tongue. In this way, the basic requirements for an eventual return to the land of origin are safeguarded.

To fulfil both these tasks, Instruction for Children of Foreign Workers is provided alongside normal lessons. They include:

- preparatory classes
- classes in which instruction is given in the mother tongue or German
- intensive courses
- remedial courses.

This instruction is, wherever possible, tailor-made to regional requirements. Although well-meant and often highly effective, there can be several drawbacks.

- The education authorities are not able to supply additional instruction in all languages for all ethnic groups and at all age and achievement levels. You may find there is none for children from your country.

- Courses cannot be held everywhere, and if you live in a small village it can be difficult or impossible for your children to get to the courses.

- Your children may hate going to additional lessons while their classmates enjoy themselves playing football. Or they may feel overburdened by having to cope with an additional curriculum.

Find out what is available, and if the courses offered are suitable for your children's requirements, make use of the service.

UNIVERSITIES AND POLYTECHNICS

To gain admission to a polytechnic, you need to have attended at least year 12 at a Gymnasium. To study at a university, you must have completed the 13-year Gymnasium education and passed the Abitur examination. UK A levels, although achieved at a much younger age and therefore less comprehensive education, are usually accepted, because they are the highest secondary education available in the UK. British nationals are usually all right if they take a university course on a subject they studied for A levels, but may find it difficult if they take other courses.

For some courses, there are more applicants than places (for example, medicine), and a special selection system is in operation. It is usually easier to find places in scientific and engineering subjects than in arts courses.

German university courses last longer than in most other countries. You usually do a *Grundstudium* for two years, during which students cover approximately the same ground as in the UK for a BA degree, but then have to do another four or six years before they awarded their university degree *(Diplom)*.

With thirteen years at school and six or more years at university, most students are between 25 and 30 years old when they graduate from university. They are highly qualified and very knowledgeable. But their skills, talents and labour are withheld form the German economy for several years during which other countries make full use of their young graduates.

Although university and polytechnic courses are free, accommodation can be costly. Rooms in university halls are reasonably priced, but there are not enough available. If money is a problem (and it is for most German students, too, especially because of the long duration of their studies), apply for a place at a university in a town rather than a city. Rents are likely to be lower.

Information: Hochschulrektorenkonferenz (The University Rectors' Conference), Ahrstr. 395, 53175 Bonn, Germany.

PRIVATE COLLEGES

As an alternative to a state college, you can study at a private college. In fact, there are qualifications for which you cannot prepare at a state college, for example practitioner of homeopathy, masseur, secretary or bilingual secretary (however, if you can acquire the necessary skills in another way, you can sit for the public examinations without attending a college at all).

Realschule or A level education is the usual entry requirement. But be warned: private colleges tend to be costly. When calculating the overall cost of the course, take into account the accommodation.

If you enrol with a view to a full-time career in Germany, select courses which lead to a recognised qualification, if possible one which begins with *'staatlich geprüft'* or *'staatlich anerkannt'*.

If, on the other hand, you want to study mainly out of personal interest, or to gain additional skills, public recognition of the certificate is less important.

Here is a selection of courses and organisers:

Euro-Schulen-Organisation, Haupstr. 26B, D-63811 Stockstadt, Germany. Tel: (06027) 4 1880. A variety of courses for bilingual secretaries with *'staatlich geprüft'* certificate.

Modefachschule Sigmaringen, D-72482 Sigmaringen, Germany. Tel: (07571) 7401-0. Fashion design.

Berufsfachschule Norkauer, Prielmayerstr. 1, D-80335 München, Germany. Tel: (089) 591693. Beautician.

Merkur-Akademie, Amalienstr. 81, D-76133 Karlsruhe, Germany. Tel: (0721) 258 71. Bilingual secretary.

Deutsche Paracelsus Schulen für Naturheilverfahren GmbH, Sonnenstr. 19r, D-80331 München, Germany. Tel: (089) 552541-38. Homeopathy.

Berufsfachschule für Mode und industrielle Fertigungstechnik. Gaisburgstr. 4, D-70182 Stuttgart, Germany. Tel: (0711) 23699648. Fashion design and textile manufacturing.

Wirtschaftsinstitut Baden-Baden, Laubstr. 24/L, D-76530 Baden-Baden, Germany. Tel: (07221) 66012). Bilingual secretary *(staatlich anerkannt)*.

VOCATIONAL TRAINING

Most young people serve a training period or apprenticeship when they leave school. This training is regulated by chambers of industry, trade and commerce.

There are 376 different training schemes available – from wholesale and foreign trade manager to publisher, from ladies' tailor to photographer, from dental surgery assistant to car mechanic. Some placements are difficult to get, for example office manager *(Bürokaufmann* or *Bürokauffrau)* and doctor's assistant *(Arzthelfer* or *Arzthelferin)*, because they are extremely popular with German applicants.

However, you can find training placements in retail, nursing, building and construction, and mechanics. To get a training place, you apply to a company in the relevant sector. For example, if you wish to train as a car mechanic in German, you contact car manufacturers and large garages.

Only companies which are run by, or employ, suitably qualified persons may take on trainees. For example, you can train to be a bricklayer only if your employer is (or employs) a master bricklayer who is responsible for your training.

Most training schemes last for three years. They can be shortened for people who have attended a higher secondary school. At the end of the training you pass an examination and are then a qualified car mechanic (or whatever).

During the training time, you can choose to attend part-time vocational courses, either specialist courses for your particular job, or, if no such course is available locally, for the related job description. You acquire the theoretical knowledge necessary for passing the final examination.

These courses take up one full day or two mornings per week (and count as work hours) and are optional if you are eighteen or over. For trainees under eighteen, they are obligatory.

ADULT EDUCATION

Adult education centres are called *Volkshochschulen*, and they operate in a similar way to the British adult education centres. You can learn, at reasonable cost, various skills which are useful for health, leisure or professional interests. Anything goes from yoga to belly dancing, from basic Mandarin Chinese to advanced Russian, from painting watercolour landscapes to exploring the medieval history of the town. Remember that small towns and villages offer a limited variety of courses, compared to large cities.

If the course helps you (in the widest sense) to start a new career, find a job or keep a job, keep the receipt. You may be able to claim tax relief.

New courses begin in September and in January, and course programmes can be picked up at the local offices as well as at banks and authorities such as the Einwohnermeldeamt.

Regional Volkshochschulen are organised in the German Adult Education Federation.

Address: Deutscher Volkshochschulverband e.V., Rheinallee 1, D-53173 Bonn, Germany.

CORRESPONDENCE COURSES

Correspondence courses are ideal for people who are home bound (perhaps because of a physical handicap or because they are looking after small children.) Studying by correspondence is cost- and time-effective, but you need a lot of self-discipline.

One disadvantage of correspondence courses is that you don't meet other people. But the great plus is that you may be able to start your studies while you are still in your home country. If you choose a professional skills course, this can help you acquire the terminology of the trade and possibly lead to a qualification recognised in Germany.

Of course you need excellent German to master a correspondence course. Here are a few correspondence schools:

Axel Andersson Akademie, Gesellschaft für Fernstudien mbH, Neumann-Reichardtstr. 27–33, D-22041 Hamburg 70, Germany. Foreign languages, writing, copywriting, arts, design.

Institut für Lernsysteme, Postfach 70 03 33, D-22123 Hamburg, Germany. Tel: (040) 67570-177. Computer programming, interior design, bilingual secretary, arts, *Mittlere Reife, Abitur,* business studies, foreign languages, accountant *(staatlich anerkannt)*, secretary *(staatlich anerkannt)*, tax, sales techniques, electrician, car mechanic and many more.

Fernakademie für Erwachsenenbildung, Doberaner Weg 22, D-22143 Hamburg, Germany. Fax: (040) 67 57084. Secretary *(staatlich anerkannt)*, investment advisor, computing, French, Spanish, and more.

Funkkolleg, Zentralbüro, Robert-Mayer-Str. 20, D-60486 Frankfurt 90, Germany. Programme changes. Past programmes have included arts, human ecology, media and communication studies, politics, law and health. Studies are based on radio broadcasts and correspondence.

A.F.S. Fernschule GmbH, Harscampstr. 71,35B, D-52001 Aachen, Germany. Tel: (0241) 234 13. Beautician, chiropodist.

SGD Studiengemeinschaft Darmstadt, Postfach 100164, D-64201 Darmstadt, Germany. Secretary *(staatlich anerkannt)*, languages, shorthand, sales techniques, interior design, psychology, business studies.

Gabler Sekretariat Verlag, Taunusstr. 54, Postfach 1546, D-65005 Wiesbaden, Germany. Fax: (0611) 598783. Secretary *(staatlich anerkannt)*, business studies, training skills.

USEFUL WORDS AND PHRASES

Ausbildung, Lehre   training, apprenticeship
Auszubildende/Auszubildender   female/male trainee or apprentice
berufliches Gymnasium   vocational college
Berufsschule   vocational school
Fachhochschule   polytechnic
Grundschule   primary school
Gymnasium   secondary school which lasts for nine years after completion of primary education
Mittlere Reife   exam and certificate achieved after completing the Realschule
Realschule   secondary school which lasts for six years after completion of primary education
Schulplicht   compulsory education
Universität   university
Volkshochschule   adult education centre

11
Being Green

Environmental protection, energy saving, fighting pollution, noise reduction and waste management are important issues in Germany. Much has been achieved in recent years, and Germany is probably the world leader in this field. However, there is still a lot to be done.

Environmental protection is the responsibility of individuals as well as of communities. Contribute your bit to saving nature; the Germans will expect you to.

PROBLEMS IN THE EAST

According to the *Bundesumweltministerium* (Federal Ministry of the Environment), the environment is in some cases in a catastrophic state in the new Länder. The socialist planned economy resulted in high levels of pollution. Main causes include:

- An obsolete production structure which damaged air, soil and water substantially.
- Inefficient energy provision, based mostly on lignite.
- Inadequate infrastructure, especially for transport and waste disposal.
- An agricultural system with large-scale industrial units which led to soil compaction, extreme chemical inputs, erosion, and destruction of natural biospheres.

TRAVELLING AND COMMUTING

By bicycle
Cycling is popular in Germany because it is low-cost transport, uses up no energy (except yours) and doesn't contribute to pollution. Commute by bike, and avoid traffic congestion and car park worries, save money on petrol or bus tickets, get fit, and help the environment.

There are many cycle lanes *(Radwege)* in Germany, usually between the motorists' lanes and the footpaths, so that cycling is comparatively safe even in the cities.

By train

Trains are a favoured means of transport because they are more environmentally friendly than cars. Most trains use electricity. The German railway network is good, modern and reliable, especially in the west.

If you are used to commuting on some of British Rail's lines where loudspeaker announcements such as 'this train has been cancelled due to engine problems, we regret the inconvenience' are the norm, you will be pleasantly surprised.

Germans trains are punctual. Delays are rare – and problems with the wrong type of snow or leaves on the rail are unheard of.

There are different types of trains, each identified by a letter or combination of letters (for example, D, E, IC, IR), according to distance covered, speed and comfort. For the more comfortable types of train, you have to pay a *Zuschlag* (supplementary charge). The Zuschlag is cheaper if you pay for it when you buy your ticket, than if you buy it on the train from the conductor.

By bus or underground

Bus services operate in all towns and reach most villages, although not necessarily frequently. In rural areas, you pay the driver when you enter. In towns, you may have to use a ticket machine. At the ticket machine, you can also buy multiple tickets, and you cancel one section of the ticket with the 'devaluation' machine inside the bus.

This system may seem confusing at first; ask your German fellow-passengers for help.

Most cities have an underground system. This is called *Untergrundbahn*, or U-Bahn for short, and the symbol is a white capital U on a blue background.

By car

Consider sharing a car on your way to work. This arrangement between a group of commuters is called *Mitfahrgemeinschaft.*

If you want to travel over a long distance, contact a *Mitfahrzentrale.* This is an agency which brings drivers and passengers together. This saves petrol costs for both, reduces pollution, and makes travelling more interesting. You can ask specifically for a non-smoking companion, and women can request a female driver or passenger. The agency charges a small fee.

There is a *Mitfahrzentrale* in almost every town, and several in the cities. You find them in the telephone book.

Learning to drive

Driving on the right-hand side of the road comes naturally to some drivers, others find it difficult. Most drivers are all right while they are aware of the difference, and problems arise when they leave a car park or petrol station and absent-mindedly start off in the wrong direction.

It's worth investing in a few refresher lessons with a *Fahrschule* (driving school). You may need as little as two lessons if you find you adjust easily; some drivers feel secure on the right-hand side of the road only when they have had eight or ten lessons.

Foreigners can usually drive with the driving licence from their home country for a limited period, for example one year. After that, the licence has to be exchanged for a German one, for which a fee will be charged.

If you learn to drive in Germany, you have to do it with a qualified instructor, which can be costly. You are not permitted to drive on the roads unless you hold a licence. It is not enough to take a friend with you who holds a licence.

Before you apply for a driving licence, you must attend a short course in first aid – a sensible requirement. Drivers are encouraged to repeat the course every three to five years. This is important, because in Germany you are legally obliged to give first aid if you come upon an accident. To find out about short courses in first aid, contact your local branch of the Rotes Kreuz (Red Cross) or of the *Malteser Hilfsdienst* (St John's).

Buying and owning a car

German cars (Audi, Opel, Volkswagen, Mercedes-Benz, Porsche) are probably the most reliable in the world. Unfortunately, they are also among the most expensive, even in Germany.

You can buy Italian, French or Japanese cars which are slightly cheaper. British cars are almost unheard of, and American cars are regarded as collectors' items.

You can get tax concessions if you buy a low-pollutant car and unleaded petrol.

Amongst the second-hand cars *(Gebrauchtwagen)*, a German brand is probably your best bet. Even after ten or more years, the average German car will run reliably and require little repair.

For a nearly new car, consider the *Jahreswagen* (year car) scheme. Some car manufacturers give their workers and employees a new car every year as a perk, which can be sold after a year. If you travel to a car manufacturing town, you may find a wide selection of nearly new cars in excellent condition at a very reasonable price. Ask your German friends and colleagues for advice where to go.

The TÜV *(Technischer Überwachungsverein)* is the German equivalent of the MoT, but it is much stricter. You have to take your car for a thorough check-up before you register it, and then every other year.

The equivalent of the RAC and AA is the ADAC (Allegemeiner Deutscher Automobil-Club) which has branches in most towns. Look up the local address in the phone book. It provides break-down and accident rescue, safety training, a magazine for members and other services.

Drivers are required to carry a warning triangle and a first aid kit in their cars. The first aid kit must meet specific standards and contain, among other items, plastic gloves to protect the first-aider from HIV infection. You can buy first aid kits for cars from pharmacies, car accessory shops, ADAC shops, and garages.

WASTE MANAGEMENT

On average, every person in Germany produces 360 kg of litter per year. This is slightly below the figures for some other European countries, but still ridiculous: it costs money to produce all those packages, and it costs money to dispose of them.

Germany strives to reduce the wasteload, for example by re-using packages, and to recycle waste.

Here are the most important rules for avoiding waste in the first place:

- Avoid waste wherever possible. Bring your own bag when you go shopping, and take your own plastic containers when you buy meat and cheese.

- Re-use containers, and return them to the place where you bought them, for re-use. There are extensive re-use schemes in operation, for example for glass bottles. You pay a deposit for every bottle you take out of the shop, and get it back when you return the bottle. Remember to take your empties with you each time you go shopping.

- Don't buy items with unnecessary wrapping (for example, cucumbers in cling film).

- Don't buy disposable items, such as paper plates and plastic cutlery.

Disposing of waste

Every household in Germany is obliged to collect its waste in at least three separate bins. There are separate collections, and waste materials are being recycled and re-used in an economical way.

- *The Bio bin:* This is for biodegradable kitchen waste, for example spoilt vegetables and fruit, peel, teabags, coffee filters, nutshells, fish, cheese and meat leftovers, dairy products (other than milk), leaves, grass, twigs, flowers, hair, paper tissues. Put a layer of crumpled paper on the bottom of the bin, and every three to four days add a layer of four newspaper pages to prevent wetness and smells, as the bin will be emptied only once a week.

- *The Wertstoff bin:* Depending on the local regulations, you can use it for paper, cardboard, aluminium, cans and tins, metal objects, cork, plastics, old clothes, textiles, anything bearing a 'green dot'. You may be required to deliver some of these items personally to a Wertstoffhof.

- *The Restmüll bin:* This is for ashes, diapers, photos, fat, light bulbs, rubber, tampons, rags, old leather shoes, porcelain, sweepings, toothpaste tubes, cigarette butts, wallpaper, vacuum cleaner bags, small mirrors, candles.

- In addition, there are bottle banks which are similar to those in the UK, except that their use is obligatory.

- There are also collection points for batteries, fridges, freezers, electric items, bulky items, chemicals and so on. You may be charged a fee for the disposal of these items. Before you shout that this is an outrage, consider that someone has to pay, directly or indirectly, for the disposal. Why not those who cause the waste? There is another interesting option: if you buy a new electric item, you can give the old one (free of charge) to the dealers, and leave the problem of disposal with them.

'GREEN DOTS' AND 'BLUE ANGELS'

The 'Green Dot' *(der grüne Punkt)*, a small round logo with two arrows, indicates recyclable – but not necessarily recycled – packaging. It does not mean than a product is environmentally friendly, only that the packaging should be placed in the Wertstoff bin, and that the manufacturers have agreed to pay for its disposal.

The 'Blue Angel' *(der blaue Engel)*, a round logo with a figure with spread arms and a wreath indicates that a product is certified to be environmentally friendly. Information as to how it is environmentally friendly are added to the logo. So a vacuum cleaner may be awarded a Blue Angel because it has been made from recycled materials, but it may still be far from perfect in other respects. For example, its high noise level may be damaging the environment. On the whole, however, you are safe assuming that the Blue Angel shows a product which is 'greener' than its competitors.

HOW TO BE GREEN

- Use recycled paper for your private correspondence. In business, you may gain image points by using good quality (not dark grey) recycled letterheads.

- Use as few chemicals in your household as possible. Use soft soap to clean your floors, and water with a dash of vinegar (instead of disinfectant) for your kitchen surfaces and fridge.

- Strong liquids to clear blocked drains, and artificial room fragrances are taboo.

- Use only phosphate-free detergent.

- For an effective, environment-friendly window cleaner, use warm water and add a little washing-up liquid and vinegar. Rub the windows dry with old newspapers.

- Use beeswax to protect furniture.

- To clean tiles, use clear water with a little spirit.

CASE STUDIES

Claire makes compost

'We got a waste disposal fee reduction because we made our own compost and reduced the amount of waste in the Bio bin. We had to prove that we really made compost, and fill in a couple of forms stating the size and location of our compost heap. A neighbour who has no garden also gets the reduced fee, because he produces compost in a special bin in his kitchen. He assures us it doesn't smell.'

Kevin learns to recycle

'It took me a while to get used to all those bins. I'm still tempted to throw everything into the Restmüll bin when I'm tired or in a hurry. I went on an outing to a tourist spot, and even the picnic site had three colour-coded bins. You can't escape it. But I see the point: it costs so much money to produce all the packaging materials, and even more money to destroy them. So why not re-use and recycle every bit?'

Sarah approves of 'going green'

'My au pair family provided me with my own bicycle. I used public transport a lot, and I found it not expensive at all. To my surprise I was allowed to take my bike into buses. The other surprise was that all buses leave precisely on time. In the UK, if a bus is scheduled for half past one, it will leave at quarter to two. I assumed this was the case in Germany, too, and I promptly missed my first bus!

'I saw no double-decker buses. Instead there were those long ''bendy'' buses, linked by an elastic section which allowed the long vehicles to turn around corners. The kids loved standing in that section.

'I find the German system of waste sorting brilliant. You've got three or four bins in the kitchen, for example a green one for newspapers and magazines, a black one for old food and biodegradable rubbish, a brown one for recyclable plastics and yoghurt cartons, and another one for things you don't know what to do with – for example, nappies. Most households also have a box for batteries.

'Each day, there is a collection for a different bin, for example paper on Mondays, and each collection is done by a different company. I also took re-usable bottles – yoghurt, for example – back to the supermarket to get some money back.

'I found that the system worked really well. Returning to the UK, I had a bit of a shock seeing that people don't even think about these matters. I think we should start caring more about the environment and thinking about the litter problem.'

USEFUL WORDS AND PHRASES

Auto car
Bahnhof railway station
Bus bus
Bushaltestelle bus stop
Erste Hilfe first aid
Fahrrad bicycle
Fahrschein, Fahrkarte ticket
Fahrschule driving school
Führerschein driving licence
Gebrauchtwagen second-hand car
Mitfahrgemeinschaft car share
U-Bahn underground train
Zug train
Zuschlag supplementary charge

USEFUL ADDRESSES

Allgemeiner Deutscher Fahrrad-Club e.V. (German Bicycle Club), Bundesgeschäftsstelle, Hollerallee 23, D-28209 Bremen, Germany. Tel: (0421) 346290. Fax: (0421) 3462950.

Bund für Umwelt und Naturschutz Deutschland e.V. (German Association for the protection of the environment and nature), Im Rheingarten 7, D-53225 Bonn, Germany. Tel: (0228) 400970. Fax: (0228) 4009740.

Grüne Liga e.V. (Green League), Friedrichstr. 165, D-10117 Berlin, Germany. Tel: (030) 2292990. Fax: (030) 2291822.

Naturschutzbund Deutschland e.V., Bundesgeschäftsstelle, Herbert-Rabius-Str. 26, D-53225 Bonn. Tel: (0228) 975610. Fax: (0228) 9756190.

Verkehrsclub Deutschland e.V., Eifelstr. 2, D-5311 Bonn, Germany. Tel: (0228) 985850. Fax: (0228) 444290.

12
Communicating and Doing Business

The first thing you notice is that the Germans are formal in their communication. They stick to Herr and Frau (Mr and Ms) for years, even if they have lived next door to someone or worked closely together for ten years.

CONVERSATION

First names are rarely used among colleagues or neighbours, let alone business partners. Always call them 'Herr Maier', 'Frau Müller' (or whatever their names are).

There are two German equivalents of the word 'you': *Du* and *Sie*. *Du* is used for children, relatives, classmates at school and close friends. *Sie* is for everyone aged 16 or over to whom you are not related and who doesn't go to college or university with you. You also use *Sie* for your boss, your secretary and your colleagues.

There are subtleties which can confuse the foreigner: for example, if the teenager in question is your friend's son, you may still call him *Du* even if he is sixteen. Students at the adult education college, however, call each other *Sie*.

If in doubt, stick to the *Sie*. The switch from *Du* to *Sie* is suggested by the person who is higher in rank or older.

MAKING A PHONE CALL

Even if you speak and understand German well, you may find it difficult to understand what the person on the other end of the line is saying, because you don't see the gestures and facial expressions which would help guess the meaning.

Don't be embarrassed. Just explain that you are British, Irish, American (or whatever your nationality is), and ask them to speak slowly.

The main difference to note is that in Germany the recipients of a call identify themselves immediately. It would be rude to pick up the receiver and just say 'yes?'. Give your surname, but not – for security reasons – your first names.

You can ask for your line to be ex-directory, but many expats have regretted this decision, because their relatives and friends at home could not contact them in an emergency if they did not have the number at hand. Careful Germans ask for only the surname and initials without the address to be included in the directory, and you can do the same.

International phone calls

To phone from one country to another, dial a code which indicates 'international call'. For most countries, including Germany and the UK, this code is OO.

Then dial the country code. This is a two (sometimes three) digit number, for example 49 stands for Germany, 353 for Ireland, and 44 for the UK.

This is followed by the area code, which is always printed in brackets in this book, but drop the first 0, and dial the number.

Sample private telephone conversation

Recipient:	'Schmidt.'
Caller:	'Guten Tag, hier spricht Susanne Maier. Ich möchte Klaus Schmidt sprechen, bitte.'
Recipient:	'Am Apparat.'
Caller:	'Ich rufe an, um zu fragen, ob Sie am Samstag zur Versammlung kommen.'
Recipient:	'Ja, ich werde kommen.'
Caller:	'Gut, vielen Dank, Herr Schmidt. Auf Wiederhören.'
Recipient:	'Auf Wiederhören.'

Translation

Recipient:	'Schmidt.' (his surname)
Caller:	'Good day, this is Susanne Maier. I want to speak to Klaus Schmidt, please.'
Recipient:	'Speaking.'
Caller:	'I'm phoning to ask if you will be coming to the meeting on Saturday.'
Recipient:	'Yes, I will come.'
Caller:	'Good, thank you, Mr Smith. Goodbye.'
Recipient:	'Goodbye.'

A sample business telephone call

Recipient:	'Importgesellschaft Hamburg, guten Tag.'
Caller:	'Hier spricht Susanne Maier von Außenhandelsberatung GmbH. Kann ich bitte Herrn Klaus Schmidt sprechen?'
Recipient:	'Einen Moment, bitte. Ich verbinde . . . Es tut mir leid, er nimmt nicht ab. Möchten Sie eine Nachricht hinterlassen?'
Caller:	'Nein danke, ich probiere es später noch einmal. Auf Wiederhören.'
Recipient:	'Auf Wiederhören.'

Translation

Recipient:	'Importgesellschaft Hamburg (the name of the firm), good day.'
Caller:	'This is Susanne Maier of Außenhandelsberatung GmbH (name of the firm) speaking. May I speak to Mr Klaus Schmidt, please?
Recipient:	'One moment please, I'll put you through . . . I'm sorry, there's no reply. Would you like to leave a message?'
Caller:	'No thank you, I'll try again later. Goodbye.'
Recipient:	'Goodbye.'

Directory enquiries

To enquire about a phone number within Germany, phone **01188**. For foreign phone numbers, phone **00118**. Please note: these are the numbers which are used in most parts of Germany, but there may be local differences.

If you have questions, problems, suggestions or criticism regarding the operation of the newly privatised Deutsche Telekom AG, phone **01113**.

When you've just moved into your new flat and need a phone or fax line, a new telephone or another service, ring **01114**.

For questions about mobile phones, there is an information service on **01300171**.

You will find other useful numbers – from daily recipe suggestions to cinema programmes – on the front pages of the telephone book.

Emergency numbers

In the case of a fire, phone the Feuerwehr, Tel: 112. In all other emergencies, contact 110. The switchboard staff there will pass on the call to the police, ambulance or other relevant emergency service.

WRITING A LETTER

Addresses, titles and postcodes

Begin with the title (Herrn, Frau, or a professional title) in the first line. Note that if you talk to a man, he is 'Herr Meier', if you write to him, he is 'Herrn Meier' as part of the address and 'Herr Meier' as part of the greeting. The titles Dr and Prof, however, are put in the second line before the name.

Don't use 'Fräulein' for a single woman, unless she requests it specifically. It is old-fashioned and may be taken as an insult. The literal translation for Fräulein is 'little woman', and the gender is not female, but neuter, so grammatically the Fräulein is treated as an object, not a person. In official correspondence all women, married, widowed, divorced, separated, cohabiting or single, have the title 'Frau'.

The second line contains the full name, the third the company name, followed by the department. Then comes the road, the post office box if appropriate, an empty line, the postcode and (in the same line) the village or town.

Every German address has a five-digit postcode which you write in front of the town or village. If you write to Germany from abroad, use the prefix D- before the postcode. If you find a German address with a four-digit postcode, it is probably pre-unification and outdated. You can telephone (0130) 55555 (freephone) for postcode information.

Examples

Herrn
Michael Meier
Personalabteilung
Exportberatung
Unterdorfst. 10

D-00000 Hintertupfingen
Germany

Frau
Prof Dr Susanne Schneider
Internationaler Warenverkehr GmbH
Goetheplatz 1
Postfach 00 00 00

D-00000 Oberkopfhausen
Germany

Müller & Meier Spielwaren GmbH

Hauser Str. 1, Industriegebiet, 00000 Tupfingen
Tel 0000/0000, Fax 0000/0000

1. Dezember 199X

Bauer Spiel und Sport
Z. Hd. Frau Barbara Bauer
Dorfgasse 1

00000 Tupfelsdorf

Sehr geehrte Frau Bauer,

vielen Dank für Ihr Schreiben vom 23. November. Wir freuen uns über
Ihr Interesse an unserem Spielwarenangebot.

Gern legen wir den gewünschten Prospekt und unsere aktuelle Preisliste
bei. Bitte zögern Sie nicht, uns anzurufen, wenn Sie Fragen haben. Wir
freuen uns darauf, von Ihnen zu hören.

Mit freundlichen Grüßen

Simmer

Simone Simmer
Leiterin der Vertriebsabteilung

Anlagen
Prospekt
Preisliste

Fig. 10. Sample business letter with translation.

Müller & Meier Spielwaren  GmbH

Hauser Str. 1, Industriegebiet, 00000 Tupfingen

Tel 0000/0000, Fax 0000/0000

1 December 199X

Bauer Spiel und Sport
FAO Ms Barbara Bauer
Dorfgasse 1

00000 Tupfelsdorf

Dear Ms Bauer,

Thank you for your letter of 23 November. We are pleased to hear you are interested in our range of toys and games.

We have pleasure enclosing the requested brochure and our current price list. Please don't hesitate to phone if you have any queries. We look forward to hearing from you.

Yours sincerely

Simmer

Simone Simmer
Head of distribution department

Enclosures
Brochure
Price list

Fig. 10. Continued.

How to begin the letter

'*Sehr geehrte Herren*' (Dear Sirs) is no longer used in Germany. The correct and polite way to address an unknown person, or group of people, is '*Sehr geehrte Damen und Herren*'. This is the equivalent of 'Dear Madams and Sirs', and means literally 'Much honoured ladies and gentlemen'. This address is followed by a comma, and the first sentence of the letter begins with a lower case letter.

Note that the Germans consider it a lack of politeness if the first word of a letter is 'I'. Once upon a time, Germans avoided starting any sentence with 'I' in polite correspondence, which required some grammatical acrobatics. Luckily, the rules have relaxed, and you have to pay attention only to the first sentence. This is easy if you begin with '*danke für Ihren Brief*' (thanks for your letter) or '*mit Interesse habe ich gelesen . . .*' (it is with interest that I have read . . .).

Ending the letter

The best closing phrase is '*Mit freundlichen Grüßen*' (with friendly greetings) which is sometimes used in the singular '*Mit freundlichem Gruß*'. No other form is acceptable for a business or application letter.

'*Hochachtungsvoll*' and '*Mit vorzüglicher Hochachtung*' are out-dated. They are only used if you write to a person of exceptionally high rank – say, an archbishop or a secretary of state – or if you wish to insult somebody by cynical politeness.

In private correspondence, the usual phrase is '*Viele Grüße*'.

AT THE POST OFFICE

The German postal service offers reduced rates for *Büchersendungen* (books), *Warensendungen* (merchandise) and letters to and from blind people (*Blindensendung*). A Blindensendung may be transported free of charge; ask at the counter for information. Mark the type of mail you wish to send above the address.

There is no division into first and second class mail. However, you can send your letters registered (*Einschreiben*, which costs DM 3.50 extra), insured (*Wertbrief*, which costs DM 9 extra) and special delivery (*Eilzustellung*, which costs DM 9 extra).

To speed up the procedure at the post office counter, the Postdienst requests that you:

●   Affix the stamps yourself.

- Fill in all forms with a pen before handing them in at the counter.

- When ordering large quantities of stamps, hand in a written list of quantities and values and add up the totals.

Postal rates within Germany

There are four basic letter categories:

- *Standardbrief* (standard letter). Up to 20 g, not larger than 23.5 x 12.5 cm and not thicker than 0.5 cm: DM 1.00.

- *Kompaktbrief* (compact letter). Up to 50 g, not larger than 23.5 x 12.5 cm and not thicker than 1 cm: DM 2.00.

- *Grossbrief* (large letter). Up to 500 g, not larger than 35.3 x 25.0 cm and not thicker than 2 cm: DM 3.00.

- *Maxibrief* (extra large letter). Up to 1,000 g, not larger than 35.5 x 25.0 cm and not thicker than 5 cm: DM 4.00.

Sending a parcel

For parcels, you can buy folding cardboard sets complete with parcel forms in duplicate, self-adhesive tape, and a piece of string in four sizes. These sets cost:

- Size 1, 25 x 17.5 x 10 cm: DM 4.20.

- Size 2, 35 x 25 x 12 cm: DM 4.70.

- Size 3, 40 x 25 x 15 cm: DM 5.00.

- Size 4, 50 x 30 x 20 cm: DM 5.50.

Parcel rates within Germany

Up to 5 kg	DM 7.60
5–6 kg	DM 8.20
6–7 kg	DM 8.90
7–8 kg	DM 9.30
8–9 kg	DM 10.00
9–10 kg	DM 10.40
10–12 kg	DM 11.10

12–14 kg	DM 12.70
14–16 kg	DM 14.00
16–18 kg	DM 15.30
18–20 kg	DM 16.50

For further information about postal services within Germany, contact: Zentrale Auskunftstelle für den Auslandspostdienst, Postfach 10 00 00, D-60285 Frankfurt, Germany. Tel: (0130) 804141.

Postal rates from Germany to other European countries

Standardbrief (see measurements above)	DM 1.00
Kompaktbrief (see measurements above)	DM 2.00
Maxibrief up to 50 g	DM 3.00
Maxibrief 50–100 g	DM 5.00
Maxibrief 100–250 g	DM 8.00
Maxibrief 250–500 g	DM 12.00
Maxibrief 500–750 g	DM 16.00
Maxibrief 750–1,000 g	DM 20.00
Maxibrief 1,000–1,5000 g	DM 28.00
Maxibrief 1,500–2,000 g	DM 36.00
Postcard	DM 0.80

Postal rates from Germany worldwide

Standardbrief (see measurements above)	DM 3.00
Kompaktbrief (see measurements above)	DM 4.00
Maxibrief up to 50 g	DM 6.00
Maxibrief 50–100 g	DM 10.00
Maxibrief 100–250 g	DM 16.00
Maxibrief 250–500 g	DM 24.00
Maxibrief 500–750 g	DM 32.00
Maxibrief 750–1,000 g	DM 40.00
Maxibrief 1,000–1,500 g	DM 56.00
Maxibrief 1,500–2,000 g	DM 72.00
Postcard	DM 2.80

For further information about postal services from Germany to other countries, including foreign postcodes, contact: Auskunftstelle für Postleitzahlen des Auslandes, Postfach 11 00, D-35035 Marburg, Germany. Tel: (06421) 966-435 or 966-436.

Remember that postal rates may change. Get an up-to-date leaflet from your local post office.

PUNCTUALITY

Germans value punctuality. It a meeting is scheduled for two o'clock, make sure you arrive at least five minutes early. If it is a private visit or party, you may arrive either on time or five minutes late.

Remember that the German way of giving the time is different from the English way. For example, *halb acht* (half eight) is 7.30, not 8.30. Unless you are aware of this, you may be one hour late to every event. Just to make matters more complicated, there is also *viertel acht* (quarter eight = 7.15) and *dreiviertel acht* (three-quarters eight = 7.45).

Whenever the Germans mention a time, ask them to give it in figures e.g. 'Seven thirty' = 7.30 a.m. or 'fourteen fifty' (= 2.50 p.m.).

Watch out for written figures, too. The Germans write their figure one like the British write a figure seven, and for the seven they use a cipher with an extra horizontal dash (see page 87).

The Germans use commas instead of full points for decimals. For example, half a litre is 0,51 in Germany, not 0.51. However, they use the full point to separate their thousands, millions and billions, for example 1.000.000 = 1 million.

STARTING A BUSINESS

There are over 200,000 foreign nationals in Germany who are self-employed or are running their own business. They frequently run bars, restaurants, tailoring or shoe-repair shops, travel agencies and grocery businesses. Most of them are the 'classic' type of small business, employing three to four people each.

Self-employed foreign nationals are earning about DM 28 billion per year. Most self-employed foreigners in Germany come from the following countries:

Italy (37,000)
Turkey (30,000)
Greece (23,000)
Austria (16,000)
former Yugoslavia (15,000)
Netherlands (10,000)
Great Britain (8,000)

Forms of business

You can run your business as a *Einzelunternehmung*, which is the equivalent of a sole trader. If several people are fully liable, it is an *Offene Handelsgesellschaft* (OHG for short). The equivalent of a Limited Company is either a *Gesellschaft mit beschränkter Haftung* (GmbH) or, if the shares are traded in the stock market, an *Aktiengesellschaft* (AG). There is also the form of *Kommanditgesellschaft*, where some members have full personal liability and others' liability is limited.

Pitfalls

To register your business, go to the *Gewerbeamt* or the *Amt für öffentliche Ordnung* (*Ordnungsamt* for short). In a small community, go to the Rathaus.

In Germany, you won't get permission to run a business which involves a traditional trade or craft, unless you are a master craftsman/master craftswoman yourself and have passed the relevant examination, which are demanding. However, you can get around the problem by employing someone who is a master of that trade.

Watch out for the many regulations governing what may be sold or hired out to minors. It is not allowed to sell videos, books, records, CD-ROMS, etc which glorify violence or are strongly racist. Other items may be sold, but not to people under eighteen, and not by mail order at all, and they may not be advertised.

The situation is complex and many foreign nationals have run into trouble by selling, hiring out or promoting such goods.

Remember, too, that the German law takes a strict view on opening hours of businesses. Keeping the shop open for another hour or opening on Sunday because your neighbours want to do their shopping will have disastrous consequences.

CHAMBERS OF COMMERCE

Chambers of industry and commerce are called *Industrie- und Handelskammern* (IHK for short). Here are the addresses of major chambers of industry and commerce:

IHK, Theaterstr. 6-10, Postfach 650, D-52007 Aachen, Germany. Tel: (0241) 4380. Fax: (0241) 438259.

IHK, Königstr. 18-20, D-59821 Arnsberg, Germany. Tel: (02931) 8780. Fax: (02931) 21427.

IHK, Kerschensteinerstr. 9, D-63741 Aschaffenburg, Germany. Tel: (06021) 8800. Fax: (06021) 87981.

IHK, Stettenstr. 1 u. 3, D-8650 Augsburg, Germany. Tel: (0821) 31620. Fax: (0821) 3162323.

IHK, Bahnhofstr. 25-27, D-95444 Bayreuth, Germany. Tel: (0921) 886-0. Fax: (0921) 12778.

IHK Hardenbergstr. 16-18, D-10623 Berlin, Germany. Tel: (030) 31510-0. Fax: (030) 31510278.

IHK, Niedersedlitzer Str. 63, D-01257 Dresden, Germany. Tel: (0351) 28020. Fax: (0351) 2802280.

IHK, Ernst-Schneider-Platz 1, D-40212 Düsseldorf, Germany. Tel: (0211) 35570. Fax: (0211) 3557400.

IHK, Goerdelerring 5, D-04109 Leipzig, Germany. Tel: (0341) 71530. Fax: (0341) 7153421.

TRADE FAIRS

Major international trade fair centres and their most important regular events include:

Düsseldorf
IGEDO (world fashion fair).
IGEDO (lingerie).

Address: IGDO, Kronen GMbH & Co, Danziger Str. 101, D-40468 Düsseldorf, Germany. Tel: (0211) 439601. Fax: (0211) 4396-345.

Essen
Admira (jewellery) every January and August.
Haus & Garten (living, furnishing, modernising, gardening).
Baby – Kind – Junior (children's fashion) every January or February.
IPM (gardening and flowers) every February.
Techno-Classica (veteran cars).
Equitana (equestrian sports).
Reise (tourism) every March.
Camping (camping equipment, caravans) every March.
FIBO (fitness and leisure) every April.
IFM (franchising) every June.
Häusliche Pflege (ambulatory healthcare) every autumn.
Speil (games) every October.
Motor-Show Essen (cars, motorbikes) every December.

Address: Messe Essen GmbH, Postfach 100165, D-45001 Essen, Germany. Tel: (0201) 7244-0.

Hannover

Domotex (carpets and flooring) every January.
Hannover Messe (the world's biggest industrial fair) every April.
Qualifikation (vocational training) every October.
ABF (watersports, camping, leisure) every February.
Interradio (hobby electronics and computing) every October.

Address: Deutsche Messe AG, Messegelände, D-30521 Hannover, Germany. Tel: (0511) 890. Fax: (0511) 8932626.

Nürnberg

Freizeit, Garten & Touristik (leisure, gardening, tourism) every February.
Consumenta (consumer goods, plus building and home) every autumn.

Address: AFAG-Ausstellungsgesellschaft mbH, Messezentrum D-90471, Nürnberg, Germany. Tel: (0911) 86070. Fax: (0911) 860735.

USEFUL CONTACTS FOR BUSINESS PEOPLE

British Chamber of Commerce in Germany (BCCG)

This is a private association of individuals and firms engaged or interested in British-German trade. It is financed by its members, and gives priority to serving members' interests. It provides a forum for business people in which they can meet, exchange information and share experiences. It organises seminars and workshops on problem areas, for example commercial and company law, tax and restrictive practices law, and marketing.

There is also a newsletter for members with items on forthcoming events, market developments, business opportunities, new publications, investment and trade statistics. An annual Membership Directory contains alphabetical listings and classified sections.

The BCCG is affiliated to the Association of British Chambers of Commerce and is a founder member of the Council of British Chambers of Commerce in Continental Europe.

Address: The British Chamber of Commerce in Germany, Severinstr. 60, D-50678 Köln, Germany. Tel: (0221) 314458 or 314489. Fax: (0221) 315335.

Bundesverband der Deutschen Industrie

The Bundesverband der Deutschen Industrie (BDI for short, Federation of German Industries), links together 34 member associations. In this way it can effectively represent the German industries' joint interests in dealings with policy-makers and society.

The BDI is also an interface in Europe, especially in the European Union. It is a member of the Union of Industrial and Employers' Confederations of Europe, UNICE.

Address: BDI, Gustav-Heinemann-Ufer 84-88, D-50968 Köln, Germany. Tel: (0221) 370800. Fax: (0221) 3708730.

Gfm-Getas

This market research group serves businesses, industry, government and academic institutions. It provides market and opinion surveys, advertising trial runs, image analysis, effectiveness testing for sponsorships, design display and handling tests for packages and many related services.

Address: Langelohstr. 134, D-22549 Hamburg, Germany. Tel: (040) 80096-0. Fax: (040) 80096-100.

Institut für Demoskopie Allensbach

This market research institute organises around 100 surveys and interviews around 75,000 people per year. Clients include multinational concerns. It is also renowned for its prediction of election results.

Address: D-78472 Allensbach, Germany. Tel: (07533) 8050. Fax: (07533) 3048. Contact: Frau Petra Kloske.

Nielsen

With over 1,000 staff, Nielsen collects monthly data on over 450 product groups, including hard and soft goods, and processes them into market reports. Nielsen also observes, analyses, monitors and evaluates markets to the specifications of clients.

Address: A.C. Nielsen GmbH, Ludwig-Landmann-Str. 405, D-60486 Frankfurt, Germany. Tel: (069) 7938-0. Fax: (069) 7074011.

Scriptease Redaktionsdienst

Editorial and public relations consultancy. Services include press releases, features, copy writing, exhibitions, direct mail, translations (English, German, Spanish), radio broadcasting, research. Specialist in beauty and cosmetics subjects.

Address: Im Bänkle 4, D-78343 Gaienhofen, Germany. Tel: (07735) 1787. Fax: (07735) 1297. Contact: Frau Evelyn Thomsen.

Weltsprachendienst (world language service)
This is a specialised agency for translations, also for oral interpretation from English into German, including scripts, technical, legal and scientific contexts.

Address: Bantelmann & Partner, Franklinstr. 35, D-40479 Düsseldorf, Germany. Tel: (0211) 465958. Fax: (0211) 489533 or 445127. Contact: Herr Kurt C. Bantelmann.

Zentralverband der deutschen Werbewirtschaft
In Germany, the various groups within the advertising industry are affiliated under one single organisation, Zentralverband der deutschen Werbewirtschaft (ZAW for short, German Advertising Federation). Forty organisations (which represent businesses, advertising agencies, advertising display manufacturers, advertising professionals and market research) are members.

The ZAW serves as a 'round table' for establishing a common policy and to balance the interests of all those involved in the German advertising industry, for example in controversial matters such as advertising for tobacco products, alcoholic beverages and pharmaceuticals and the portrayal of women in advertising. It also represents the advertising industry and its positions.

Address: ZAW, Villichgasse 17, D-53177 Bonn, Germany. Tel: (0228) 820920. Fax: (0227) 357583.

USEFUL WORDS AND PHRASES

Guten Tag   good day (greeting)
Guten Abend   good evening (greeting)
Guten Morgen   good morning (greeting)
Gute Nacht   good night (farewell)
Grüß Gott   be greeted in God (greeting especially in Bavaria)
Auf Wiedersehen   goodbye (person to person)

Auf Wiederhören   goodbye (on the phone)
Tschüß   goodbye (informal)
Wie geht's?   How are you?
Brief   letter
Schreiben   letter (formal)
Sehr geehrte Frau   Dear Ms
Sehr geehrter Herr   Dear Mr
Sehr geehrte Damen und Herren   Dear Madams and Sirs
Liebe Susanne   Dear Susanne (female)
Lieber Klaus   Dear Klaus (male)
z.Hd. (zu Händen)   FAO (for the attention of)
Mit freundlichen Grüssen   Yours sincerely
Viele Grüße   Best regards, best wishes
Darf ich Sie mit . . . bekanntmachen?   or **Darf ich . . .vorstellen?**
   May I introduce . . .
Darf ich mich vorstellen?   May I introduce myself?
Sehr angenehm   Pleased to meet you (formal)
Es freut mich, sie kennenzulernen   Pleased to meet you
Entschuldigung   Excuse me, I'm sorry
Danke   Thank you
Bitte   please, you're welcome
Bitte nehmen Sie Platz   Please take a seat
Bitte unterschreiben Sie hier   please sign here
Kann ich bitte . . . sprechen?   May I talk to . . ., please?
Ich verbinde   I'm putting you through
Was ist Ihre Telefaxnummer, bitte?   What's your telefax number,
   please?
Ich kann Sie nicht verstehen   I can't understand you
Bitte sprechen Sie langsam   Please speak slowly
Wie bitte?   Pardon?
Können Sie das bitte wiederholen?   Can you repeat that please?
Können Sie das bitte buchstabieren?   Can you spell it please?

Further Reading

NEWSPAPERS AND MAGAZINES

Overseas Jobs Express is a bi-weekly newspaper which not only contains lots of situations vacant advertisements (foreign employers can advertise their vacancies free of charge), but is crammed with features and advice for job-hunters, as well as personal experience reports. The author of this book is a regular contributor to the publication. Six months subscription (12 issues) £28. Overseas Jobs Express, PO Box 22, Brighton BN1 5HX, UK. Tel: (01273) 440220.

Escape – The Career Change Magazine. Bi-monthly magazine with features and advice for everyone who considers taking their career in a different direction or changing their lifestyle, including going abroad. The author of this book is a regular contributor to the publication. Annual subscription, £17.50. Weavers Press Publishing Ltd, 113 Abbotts Ann Down, Andover, Hampshire SP11 7BX.

See also pages 115-119 for German magazines.

BOOKS

A Little German Cookbook by Gertrud Philipine Matthes, with colour illustrations by Ruth Bleakley-Thiessen, published by Appletree Press. 60 pages, £3.99. Practise German cooking before you go there with the suggestions from this small book. Traditional recipes from various parts of Germany. Some of them are easy to make, others are elaborate. Some of the recipes published in this book are extracts from *A Little German Cookbook*, with the publisher's kind permission.

The series also comprises *A Little Welsh Cookbook, A Little English Cookbook, A Little Scottish Cookbook* and *A Little Irish Cookbook*, which make suitable gifts for your German friends. The Scottish and the Irish cookbook are even available in German language.

How to Get a Job in Germany, by Christine Hall, published by How To Books. 144 pages, £9.99. This book complements *How to Live & Work in Germany*. It looks closely at the job market and shows where to find vacancies. The book also provides several sample application letters and CVs in German language with English translations, and gives advice on linguist work and seasonal jobs.

Guide to Working Abroad, by Godfrey Golzen, published by Kogan Page with the *Daily Telegraph*. Paperback, 314 pages, with invaluable advice – mostly financial matters – for expatriates. Slanted at people in the higher income brackets who plan on staying long term or permanently abroad. Probably of less interest to young travellers who work their way across the world.

Teaching English Abroad – Talk Your Way Around the World, by Susan Griffith, published by Vacation Work, 9 Park End Street, Oxford, UK. Paperback, 320 pages. This useful guide for language teachers is arranged in two invaluable parts. The first gives plenty of information about qualifications, rewards, risks and job-hunting; the second is a country-by-country guide of potential employers with full addresses, stating job descriptions, working conditions and payment. There is a long chapter on Germany.

Summer Jobs Abroad, edited by David Woodworth and Giles Smart, published by Vacation Work, 9 Park End Street, Oxford, UK. This annual guide gives some information on how to apply for a job, visas, residence and work permits, au pair work, etc. But the best part of the book is the country-by-country guide of actually available summer (and winter) jobs, complete with addresses, required language skills and experience, payment, accommodation, expected duration of stay, etc. Most vacancies listed are in the hotel and catering sector, e.g. chambermaids, waiters/waitresses and kitchen assistants. If you plan on working your way around Europe and want to stay several weeks or months in Germany, this is the book for you. Make sure you have the latest copy – the information is updated every year.

Xenophobe's Guide to The Germans, by Stefan Zeidenitz and Ben Barkow, published by Ravette Books, Egmont House, 8 Clifford Street, London W1X 1RB. Paperback, 64 pages. At £2.50, this book is cheap, compact and lightweight enough for any rucksack or hand luggage, and it provides entertaining reading for the journey! The contents are hilarious as well as informative – you will truly understand the German way of living and thinking, as well as have a really good laugh.

Travellers Survival Kit Europe by David Woodworth, published by Vacation Work, 9 Park End Street, Oxford, UK. Paperback, 288 pages. Especially useful for the traveller across many European countries. Lots of advice on public transport, foreign currency, youth and student travel, communications, accommodation, etc. It contains a country-by-country guide with information and addresses which includes Germany.

European Information Pocket Book, published by NTC Publications Ltd, PO Box 69, Henley-on-Thames, Oxfordshire RG9 1GB, UK. Paperback, 224 pages. An incredible wealth of information for such a compact book. It contains, for example, not only all the embassies and chambers of commerce of all European countries, but the addresses of statistical offices, marketing and advertising associations, market research associations, television and radio organisations, publishing organisations, exhibition organisers, advertising data sources, maps, airlines, airports, train and ferry information, telephone codes and emergency numbers. An updated issue is published annually.

Facts about Germany, published by Societäts-Verlag, available through the German Embassy. A 500-page strong paperback, crammed with facts about German geography, economy, politics and so on, illustrated with colour photos. Well written and informative, highly recommended.

These Strange German Ways, by Susan Stern, published by Atlantik-Brücke e.V., Postfach 1147, D-53001 Bonn, Germany. Tel: (0228) 214160. Fax: (0228) 214659. Entertaining paperback, covering everything from 'Sentimentality, Animals and Babies' to the Oktoberfest and 'Other Reasons To Celebrate'. A good laugh, but written with an American readership in mind. If you are European, and therefore accustomed to European ways, you may find some sections less funny and even useless as far as information is concerned. For example, the absence of cheerleading will not strike you as particularly remarkable.

DIRECTORIES

Headhunters Guides, published by Avotek Publishers, PO Box 38141, NL-6503 AC Nijmegen, Netherlands. Annually updated directories for

Germany (west), Germany (north and east), Germany (south), engineers (Europe). Contain the addresses of most recruitment agencies in the relevant geographical area.

BROCHURES

Working in Germany and *Working Abroad*, both available free from job centres in the UK, or from The Employment Service, Overseas Placing Unit, Rockingham House, 123 West Street, Sheffield S1 4ER, UK.

Information on Travel in Germany, 26 pages packed with advice and addresses on almost anything a traveller might want to know, including what vaccinations are needed for your pet, the opening hours of hair-dressing establishments, phone cards, speed limits, Sunday return train tickets, cycling tours . . . Available free (but A5 s.a.e. or contribution towards postage is appreciated) from the German National Tourist Office, Nightingale House, 65 Curzon Street, London W1 7PE, UK.

Inclusive Holiday Digest, compiled by the German National Tourist Office. Contains addresses of tour organisers, arranged by type and purpose of travel.

Unsere Steuern von A-Z. An encyclopeadia of German taxes and tax-related terms, including historical annotations, in German language. Available through the German Embassy.

Health Care in Germany. Published by the German Health Ministry. With 71 pages in English language, illustrated in colour throughout, this publication is designed to show the German health service in a glowing light. You may find it a bit wordy, and you may not find the informa-tion you are really looking for, at least not at a glance. But the book is nicely laid out and it is free. Available through the German Embassy.

Soziale Sicherheit. This A4 guide through the maze of social security in Germany is illustrated with colour photos throughout. It explains the basics of housing benefits, rights and benefits for mothers, study grants and so on. A good starting point. Available (in German language) through the German Embassy.

Sozial-Report: The Statutory Health Insurance Scheme. 10 page report (printed on recycled paper) on the basics of the German health service, in English langauge. Includes a useful glossary of German expressions with their English translations. Available free from the German Embassy.

International Placement Service. A brief guide in English language on services available from the Arbeitsamt, e.g. short term work experience and graduate placements. Available free from ZAV, International Department, Feuerbachstr. 42-46, D-60325 Frankfurt am Main, Germany.

Arbeit und Aufenthalt in Deutschland. Brief guide in German language for EU nationals who wish to live and work in Germany. Covers pets, jobhunting, rights and duties, social security. Free from ZAV, (address as above).

Merkblatt für ausländische Studentinnen und Studenten – Ferienarbeit in der Bundesrepublik Deutschland. Brief guide for students seeking holiday jobs in Germany. Free from ZAV (address as above).

Glossary of German Terms

Abitur higher education examination and school-leaving certificate, similar to A levels but covers more subjects and is therefore taken by students at a slightly older age (at about 20)

Abteilungsleiter/Abteilungsleiterin male/female head of department

Arbeitgeber employer(s)

Arbeitnehmer employee(s)

Arbeitsamt a branch of, or a short word for, the Zentralstelle für Arbeitsvermittlung

Arbeitserlaubnis work permit (not necessary for EU nationals)

Arbeitsvermittlungsagenturen recruitment agencies (must be licensed by the state)

Aufenthaltserlaubnis residence permit

Ausbildung training or apprenticeship, lasts around three years; combines practical work and college studies, strictly regulated and examined by chambers of commerce

Betriebsrat shop steward

Bewerber/Bewerberin male/female applicant

Bewerbung application

Diplom university degree

Einwohnermeldeamt the authority where you have to register when taking up residence in Germany

Formular form

Freiwilliges Soziales Jahr one year of voluntary work for young people, usually in hospitals

Lebenslauf CV

Mittlere Reife secondary school education examination and school-leaving certificate, taken at the age of about 16

Sachbearbeiter/Sachbearbeiterin executive, manager (lower management)

Sozialversicherung social security

Stellenangebote situations vacant advertisements

Stellengesuche situations wanted advertisements

Tarifvertrag collective agreement about wages and working conditions in a particular industry sector, negotiated by the trade unions and the employers

Urlaubsanspruch annual leave entitlement

Zeitarbeit temporary work

Zentralstelle für Arbeitsvermittlung the German state employment service

Useful Addresses

ANGLO-GERMAN FRIENDSHIP

Anglo-German Association, 17 Bloomsbury Square, London WC1A 2LP, UK. Tel: (0171) 831 8696.

Anglo-German Club, PO Box 427, London W8 5QU, UK.

Anglo-German Club e.V., Harvestehuder Weg 44, D-20149 Hamburg, Germany. Tel: (040) 450155-12/13. Fax: (040) 447774.

Deutsch-Englische Gesellschaft e.V., Beethovenplatz 6, D-53115 Bonn, Germany. Tel: (0228) 657178. Fax: (0228) 659887.

Deutsch-Englische Gesellschaft, c/o European Business Programme, Fachhochschule Münster, Postfach 3020, D-48016 Münster, Germany. Tel: (0251) 835622. Fax: (0251) 835623.

Deutsch-Englische Gesellschaft, c/o Deutsche Bank AG, Frau Gubo, Taunusanlage 12, D-60262 Frankfurt, Germany. Tel: (069) 910-33042.

Deutsch-Englische Gesellschaft, c/o Vereins- und Westbank, Frau Könnicke, Otto von Guericke-Str. 27/28, D-39104 Magdeburg, Germany. Tel: (0391) 568530.

Deutsch-Englische Gesellschaft, Barstenkamp 35, D-24113 Molfsee, Germany. Tel: (0431) 331971.

Deutsch-Englische Gesellschaft, c/o Schulungscenter Foley, Poststr. 3, D-79098 Freiburg, Germany. Tel: (0761) 387900. Fax: (0761) 3879038.

Deutsch-Englische Gesellschaft, c/o Institut für Anglistik, Friedrich-Schiller-Universität Jena, UHH/23.OG, D-07740 Jena, Germany. Tel: (03641) 6/30902.

Deutsch-Englische Gesellschaft, Postfach 106013, D-70049 Stuttgart, Germany.

Deutsch-Englische Gesellschaft e.V., Arbeitskreis Essen, Wolfskuhle 9, D-45529 Hattingen-Niederwenigern, Germany. Tel: (02324) 43786.

Deutsch-Englische Gesellscahft München e.V., Postfach 340147, D-

80098 München, Germany. Tel: (089) 2302-2242. Fax: (089) 2302-2749.

Deutsch-Englische Gesellschaft Oldenburg, Lindenallee 65, D-26122 Oldenburg, Germany. Tel: (0441) 776552.

Internationaler Jugendaustausch und Besucherdienst der Bundesrepublik Deutschland e.v., (International Youth Exchange and Visitor Service of the Federal Republic of Germany), Hochkreuzallee 20, D-53175 Bonn, Germany.

Munich Scottish Association (promotes Scottish culture and dance), Norman Scobie, Dorfstr. 3, D-820124 Taufkirchen, Germany. Tel: (089) 6128218.

Overseas Twinning Department, c/o Local Government International Bureau, 35 Great Smith Street, London SW1P 3BJ, UK. Tel: (0171) 222 1636.

BANKING, INSURANCE, SOCIAL SECURITY

AOK Bundesverband, Kortrijker Str. 1, D-53177 Bonn, Germany. Tel: (0228) 843-309. Fax: (0228) 843 507.

BHW Bausparkasse, Postfach 10 13 22, D-31763 Hameln, Germany.

DAK, Deutsche Angestellten Krankenkasse, Nagelsweg 27-35, D-20097 Hamburg, Germany. Tel: (040) 23961409. Fax: (040) 23962219.

DBV Versicherungen, Berliner Str. 170-172, D-63014 Offenbach, Germany. Fax: (040) 98248777.

Deutsche Bundesbank, Wilhelm-Epstein-Str 14, D-60431 Frankfurt, Germany. Tel: (069) 95661. Fax: (069) 5601071.

DKV Deutsche Krankenversicherung AG, Aachener Str. 300, D-50933 Köln, Germany. Tel: (0221) 578-0. Fax: (0221) 5783694.

Deutscher Sparkassen- und Girobank e.V., Simrockstr. 4, D-53113 Bonn, Germany. Tel: (0228) 2040. Fax: (0228) 204250.

Deutsche Girozentrale, Deutsche Kommunalbank e.V., Postfach 110542, D-60040 Frankfurt, Germany. Tel: (069) 26930. Fax: (069) 2693490.

Bundesverband der Deutschen Volksbanken und Raiffeisenbanken e.V., Postfach 1204, D-53046 Bonn, Germany. Tel: (0228) 5090. Fax: (0228) 509201.

Bundesverband Deutscher Banken e.V., Kattenburg 1, D-50667 Köln, Germany. Tel: (0221) 16630. Fax: (0221) 166322.

Bundesversicherungsanstalt für Angestellte, Berlin-Wilmersdorf, Ruhrstr. 2, D-10704 Berlin, Germany.

KKH, Kaufmännische Krankenkasse, Indenburgstr. 43-45, D-30175 Hannover, Germany. Tel: (0511) 2802-213. Fax: (0511) 2802-232.

Techniker Krankenkasse, Hauptverwaltung, Bramfelder Str. 140, D-22305 Hamburg, Germany.

BUSINESS CONTACTS

Accountants Group in Germany e.V., Paul C. Hubbard. c/o KPMG Deutsche Treuhand-Gesellschaft AG, Marie-Curie-Str. 30, D-60439 Frankfurt, Germany. Tel: (069) 9586. Fax: (069) 9587-2532.

AFAG-Ausstellungsgesellschaft mbH (trade fairs), Messezentrum, D-90471 Nürnberg, Germany. Tel: (0911) 86070. Fax: (0911) 860735.

Ausstellungs- und Messeauschuss der Deutschen Wirtschaft (German Council of Trade Fairs and Exhibitions), Lindenstr. 8, D-50674 Köln, Germany.

Bundesverband des Deutschen Groß- und Außenhandels, (Federation of German Wholesale and Foreign Trade), Kaiser-Friedrich-Str. 13, D-53113 Bonn, Germany.

Bundesverband der Deutschen Industrie (Federation of German Industries), Gustav-Heinemann-Ufer 84-88, D-50968 Köln, Germany. Tel: (0221) 370800. Fax: (0221) 3708730.

Bundesverband der Deutschen Zeitungsverleger (Federation of German Newspaper Publishers), Reimenschneiderstr. 10, D-53115 Bonn, Germany.

Deutsche Messe AG (trade fairs), Messegelände, D-30521 Hannover, Germany. Tel: (0511) 890. Fax: (0511) 8932626.

GFM-GETAS (market research), Langelohstr. 134, D-22549 Hamburg, Germany. Tel: (040) 80096-0. Fax: (040) 80096-100.

Institut für Demoskopie Allensbach (market research), D-78472 Allensbach, Germany. Tel: (07533) 8050. Fax: (07533) 3048.

Institute of Directors, European Centre, Sec: Mr Dieter Feige, c/o Feige Business Advisors GmbH, Niederkasseler Str. 2, D-40547 Düsseldorf, Germany. Tel: (0211) 55734-0. Fax: (0211) 554473.

Messe Essen GmbH (trade fairs), Postfach 100165, D-45001 Essen, Germany. Tel: (0201) 7244-0.

A.C. Nielsen GmbH (market research). Ludwig-Landmann-Str. 405, D-60486 Frankfurt, Germany. Tel: (069) 7938-0. Fax: (069) 7074011.

Scriptease Redaktionsdienst (public relations consultancy), Frau Evelyn Thomsen, Im Bänkle 4, D-78343 Gaienhofen, Germany. Tel: (07735) 1787. Fax: (07735) 1297.

Verband Deutscher Zeitschriftenverleger (Association of German Periodical Publishers), Winterstr. 50, D-53177 Bonn, Germany.

Weltsprachendienst (translation service), Bantelmann & Partner, Franklinstr. 35, D-40479 Düsseldorf, Germany. Tel: (0211) 465958. Fax: (0211) 489533 or 445127.

Zentralverband der Deutschen Werbewirtschaft (German Advertising Federation), Villichgasse 17, D-53177 Bonn, Germany. Tel: (0228) 820920. Fax: (0227) 357583.

Zentralverband des Deutschen Handwerks (Federation of German Crafts and Trades), Johanniterstr. 1, D-53113 Bonn, Germany.

EDUCATION

A.F.S. Fernschule GmbH, Harscampstr. 71, 35B, D-52001 Aachen, Germany. Tel: (0241) 243 13.

Axel Andersson Akademie, Gesellschaft für Fernstudien mbH, Neumann-Reichardtstr. 27-33, D-22041 Hamburg 70, Germany.

Berufsfachschule für Mode und industrielle Fertigungstechnik, Gaisburgstr. 4, D-70182 Stuttgart, Germany. Tel: (0711) 23699648.

Berufsfachschule Norkauer, Prielmayerstr. 1, D-80335 München, Germany. Tel: (089) 591693.

Deutsche Paracelsus Schulen für Naturheilverfahren GmbH, Sonnenstr. 19r, D-80331 München, Germany. Tel: (089) 552541-38.

Deutscher Akademischer Austauschdienst (German Academic Exchange Service), Kennedyallee 50, D-53175 Bonn, Germany.

Deutscher Volkshochschulverband e.V., (German Adult Education Federation), Rheinallee 1, D-53173 Bonn, Germany.

Europäische Schule München, Elise-Aulinger-Str. 21, D-81739 München, Germany. Tel: (089) 6372611. Fax: (089) 6378418.

Euro-Schulen-Organisation, Hauptstr. 26B, D-63811 Stockstadt, Germany. Tel: (06027) 41880.

Fernakademie für Erwachsenenbildung, Doberaner Weg 22, D-22143 Hamburg, Germany. Fax: (040) 67 57084.

Funkkolleg, Zentralbüro, Robert-Mayer-Str. 20, D-60486 Frankfurt 90, Germany.

Gabler Sekretariat Verlag, Taunusstr. 54, Postfach 1546, D-65005 Wiesbaden, Germany. Tel: (0611) 534-0. Fax: (0611) 598783.

Hochschulrektorenkonferenz (The University Rectors' Conference), Ahrstr. 395, D-53175 Bonn, Germany.

Institut für Lernsysteme, Postfach 73 03 33, D-22123 Hamburg, Germany. Tel: (040) 67570-177.

Merkur-Akademie, Amalienstr. 81, D-76133 Karlsruhe, Germany. Tel: (0721) 258 71.

Modefachschule Sigmaringen, D-72482 Sigmaringen, Germany. Tel: (07571) 7401-0.

SGD Studiengemeinschaft Darmstadt, Postfach 100164, D-64201 Darmstadt, Germany.

Wirtschaftsinstitut Baden-Baden, Laubstr. 24/L, D-76530 Baden-Baden, Germany. Tel: (07221) 66012.

EMBASSIES

Deutsche Botschaft/German Embassy, 23 Belgrave Square, London SW1X 8PZ, UK. Tel: (0171) 235 5033.

Britische Botschaft/British Embassy, Friedrich-Ebert-Allee 77, D-53113 Bonn, Germany. Tel: (0228) 234061.

Deutsche Botschaft/German Embassy, 31 Trimleston Avenue, Booterstown, Co. Dublin, Ireland. Tel: (01) 2693946.

Irische Botschaft/Irish Embassy, Godesberger Allee 119, D-53175 Bonn, Germany. Tel: (0228) 376937.

GOETHE-INSTITUT BRANCHES

German Headquarters: Goethe-Institut, Zentrale Einschreibung, Helene-Weber-Allee 1, D-80604 München, Germany. Tel: (089) 15921-200/206. Fax: (089) 15921-200/202.

Goethe-Institut London, 50 Princes Gate, Exhibition Road, London SW7 2PH, UK. Tel: (0171) 411 3400.

Goethe-Institut Glasgow, 3 Park Circus, Glasgow G3 6AX, UK. Tel: (0141) 332 2555.

Goethe-Institut Manchester, 4th Floor, Churchgate House, 56 Oxford Street, Manchester M1 6EU. Tel: (0161) 237 1077.

Goethe-Institut York, The King's Manor, Exhibition Square, York YO1 2EP, UK. Tel: (01904) 611122.

Goethe-Institut Dublin, 37 Merrion Square, Dublin 2, Ireland. Tel: (01) 61155/56.

LANGUAGE SCHOOLS

Albert-Ludwigs-Universität Freiburg, Rektorat, Akademisches Auslandsamt, D-79085 Freiburg, Germany. Tel: (0761) 203-0. Fax: (0761) 203-4377.

Berlitz, 9-13 Grosvenor Street, London W1A 3BZ, UK. Tel: (0171) 915 0909. Fax: (0171) 915 0222.

CESA Languages Abroad, Western House, Malpas, Truro TR1 1SQ, UK. Tel: (01872) 225300. Fax: (01872) 225400.

DID Deutsch Institut, Hauptverwaltung, Hauptstr. 26, D-63811 Stockstadt, Germany. Tel: (06027) 447710. Fax: (06027) 417741.

Euro Academy Outbound, 77a George Street, Croydon CR0 1LD, UK. Tel: (0181) 686 2363.

Goethe-Institut, Zentrale Einschreibung, Helene-Weber-Allee 1, D-

80604 München, Germany. Tel: (089) 15921-200/206. Fax: (089) 15921-200/202.

Horizonte, Rote Hahnengasse 12, D-93047 Regensburg, Germany. Tel: (0941) 57207. Fax: (0941) 562862.

Kapito, Salzstr. 21, Postfach 8672, D-48046 Münster, Germany. Tel: (0251) 511174. Fax: (0251) 46144.

Linguaphone, St Giles House, 50 Poland Street, London W1V 4AX, UK. Tel: (0171) 287 4050. Fax: (0171) 287 1656.

Universität Regensburg, Lehrgebiet Deutsch als Fremdsprache, Universitätsstr. 31, D-93053 Regensburg, Germany. Tel: (0941) 9432425 (mornings only). Fax: (0941) 9432410.

Universität Trier, Akademisches Auslandsamt, Universitätsring 15, D-54286 Trier, Germany. Tel: (0651) 201 2806-09. Fax: (0651) 201 3914.

LEISURE INTEREST ORGANISATIONS

Bundesvereinigung Kulturelle Jugendbildung (Federation of Youth Cultural Associations), Küppelnstein 34, D-42857 Remscheid, Germany.

Deutsche Gesellschaft für Freizeit (German Leisure Association), Bahnstr. 4, D-40699 Erkrath, Germany.

Deutscher Sportbund (The German Sports Federation), Otto-Fleck-Schneise 12, D-60528 Frankfurt, Germany.

Deutsche Sportjugend (Federation of German Youth Sports Associations), Otto-Fleck-Schneise 12, D-60528 Frankfurt, Germany.

POLITICAL PARTIES

Bündnis 90/Die Grünen, Colmantstr. 36, D-53115 Bonn, Germany.

Christlich Demokratische Union Deutschlands (CDU), Konrad-Adenauer-Haus, Friedrich-Ebert-Allee 73-75, D-53113 Bonn, Germany.

Christlich-Soziale Union in Bayern (CSU), Nymphenburger Str. 64-66, D-80335 München, Germany.

Freie Demokratische Partei (FDP), Thomas-Dehler-Haus, Baunscheidtstr. 15, D-53113 Bonn, Germany.

Partei des Demokratischen Sozialismus (PDS), Bundeshaus, Görrestr. 15, D-58113 Bonn, Germany.

Sozialdemokratische Partei Deutschlands (SPD), Erich-Ollenhauer-Haus, Ollenhauerstr. 1, D-53113 Bonn, Germany.

PROFESSIONAL ASSOCIATIONS AND TRADE UNIONS

Börsenverein des Deutschen Buchhandels (The German Book Trade Association), Grosser Hirschgraben 17-21, D-60311 Frankfurt, Germany.

Bund Deutscher Sekretärinnen e.V., Zentnerstr. 44, D-80796 München, Germany. Tel: (089) 2716873. Fax: (089) 2724285.

Bundesverband Deutscher Zeitungsverleger (Federation of German Newspaper Publishers), Riemenschneiderstr. 10, D-53175 Bonn, Germany.

Christlicher Gewerkschaftsbund Deutschlands (Christian Trade Union Federation), Konstantinstr. 13, D-53179 Bonn, Germany.

Deutsche Angestelltengewerkschaft (German Union of Salaried Employees), Karl-Muck-Platz 1, D-20355 Hamburg, Germany.

Deutscher Bauernverband (German Farmers' Association) Godesberger Allee 142-148, D-53175 Bonn, Germany.

Deutscher Beamtenbund (German Civil Servants' Federation), Dreizehnmorgenweg 36, D-53179 Bonn, Germany.

Deutscher Bühnenverein (German Theatre Association), Quatermarkt 5, D-50667 Köln, Germany.

Deutscher Fremdenverkehrsvernband e.V., (Tourist Industry Association), Niebuhstr. 16b, D-53113 Bonn, Germany.

Deutscher Gewerkschaftsbund (German Trade Union Federation), Hans-Böckler-Str. 39, D-40476 Düsseldorf, Germany. Tel: (0211) 430100. Fax: (0211) 4301471.

Deutscher Journalistenverband (German Journalists Association), Bennauerstr. 60, D-53115 Bonn, Germany.

DJV-Hilfsverein (journalists' association), Regine Sakowsky, Bennauerstr. 60, D-53115 Bonn, Germany. Tel: (228) 222976. Fax: (0228) 214917.

IG Medien (Print Media Trade Union), Friedrichstr. 15, D-70174 Stuttgart, Germany.

Journalisten helfen Journalisten e.V. (journalists' initiative), Christiane Schlötzer-Sootland, Frauenstr. 12, D-80469 München, Germany. Tel./Fax: (089) 223667.

Medien gegen Rassismus (journalists' movement against racism), Ralf Radler, Medienfabrik, Hans-Böckler-Str. 163, D-50354 Köln, Germany. Tel: (0221) 456-2753. Fax: (0221) 456-2795.

Spitzenorganisation der Filmwirtschaft (Central Organisation of the Film Industry), Langenbeckstr. 9, D-65205 Wiesbaden, Germany.

Verband Deutscher Drehbuchautoren (German script writers' association), Rosenthaler Str. 39, D-10178 Berlin, Germany. Tel: (030) 2824205. Fax: (030) 2823700.

Verband Deutscher Zeitschriftenverleger (Association of German Magazine Publishers), Winterstr. 50, D-53177 Bonn, Germany.

Vereinigung Deutscher Reisejournalisten (German travel journalists' association), Gollenstr 25, D-73733 Esslingen, Germany. Tel: (0711) 378007. Fax: (0711) 378040.

RECRUITMENT AGENCIES

OCC Computer Personnel, 108 Welsh Row, Nantwich, Cheshire CW5 5EY, UK. Tel: (01270) 627206. Fax: (01270) 629168.

Solihull Au Pair & Nanny Agency, 1565 Stratford Road, Hall Green, Birmingham B28 9JA, UK. Tel: (0121) 733 644. Fax: (021) 733 6555.

South Eastern Au Pair Bureau, 39 Rutland Avenue, Thorpe Bay, Essex SS1 2XJ, UK. Tel: (01702) 601911.

STATE EMPLOYMENT ORGANISATIONS

The Employment Service, Overseas Placing Unit, Rockingham House, 123 West Street, Sheffield S1 4ER, UK. Tel: (0114) 259 6051. Fax: (0114) 259 6040.

Zentralstelle für Arbeitsvermittlung, Feuerbachstr. 42-46, D-60325 Frankfurt, Germany. Tel: (069) 71110. Fax: (069) 7111-540.

TRADE COUNCILS AND CHAMBERS OF COMMERCE

The British Council, Hahnenstr. 6, D-50667 Köln, Germany. Tel: (0221) 206 4433. Fax: (0221) 206 4455.

The British Council, Lumumbastr. 11-13, D-04105 Leipzig, Germany. Tel: (0341) 564 7153. Fax: (0341) 564 7152.

The British Council, Hardenbergstr. 20, D-10623 Berlin, Germany. Tel: (030) 311 0990. Fax: (030) 311 09920.

British Chamber of Commerce in Germany, Severinstr. 60, D-50678 Köln, Germany. Tel: (0221) 314458 or 314489. Fax: (0221) 315335.

German Chamber of Industry and Commerce, 16 Buckingham Gate, London SW1E 6LB, UK. Tel: (0171) 235 5033.

German-Irish Chamber of Industry and Commerce, 46 Fitzwilliam Square, Dublin 2, Ireland. Tel: (01) 762934.

IHK, Postfach 3440, D-76020 Karlsruhe, Germany. Tel: (0721) 174-0. Fax: (071) 174-290.

IHK, Theaterstr. 6-10, Postfach 650, D-52007 Aachen, Germany. Tel: (0241) 4380. Fax: (0241) 438259.

IHK, Königstr. 18-20, D-59821 Arnsberg, Germany. Tel: (02931) 8780. Fax: (02931) 21427.

IHK, Kerschensteinerstr. 9, D-63741 Aschaffenburg, Germany. Tel: (06021) 8800. Fax: (06021) 87981.

IHK, Stettenstr. 1 u. 3, D-8650 Augsburg, Germany. Tel: (0821) 31620. Fax: (0821) 3162323.

IHK, Bahnhofstr. 25-27, D-95444 Bayreuth, Germany. Tel: (0921) 886-0. Fax: (0921) 12778.

IHK, Hardenbergstr. 16-18, D-10623 Berlin, Germany. Tel: (030) 31510-0. Fax: (030) 31510278.

IHK, Niedersedlitzer Str. 63, D-01257 Dresden, Germany. Tel: (0351) 28020. Fax: (0351) 2802280.

IHK, Ernst-Schneider-Platz 1, D-40212 Düsseldorf, Germany. Tel: (0211) 35570. Fax: (0211) 3557400.

IHK, Goerdelerring 5, D-04109 Leipzig, Germany. Tel: (0341) 71530. Fax: (0341) 7153421.

WORK AND TRAINING RELATED INSTITUTIONS

The Comparability Coordinator/Training, Enterprise and Education Directorate, Department of Employment, Moorfoot, Sheffield S1 4PQ, UK. Tel: (0114) 2753275. Fax: (0114) 2758316/594724.

National Council for Vocational Qualifications, 222 Euston Road, London NW1 2BZ, UK. Tel: (0171) 3879898. Fax: (0171) 3870978.

TRAVEL AND ACCOMMODATION

German National Tourist Office, Nightingale House, 65 Curzon Street, London W1Y 7PE, UK. Fax: (0171) 4956129.

Deutsche Zentrale für Tourismus, Beethovenstr. 69, D-60325 Frankfurt, Germany. Tel: (069) 757 20. Fax: (069) 751903.

Deutsches Jugendherbergswerk, Hauptverband für Jugendwandern und Jugendherbergen e.V., Bismarckstr. 8, Postfach 1455, D-32754 Detmold, Germany. Tel: (05231) 7401-0. Fax: (05231) 7401-49.

DER Travel Service, 18 Conduit Street, London W1 9TD, UK. Tel: (0171) 499 0577.

German Federal Railway, Suite 118 Hudson's Place, Victoria Station, London SW1 1JL, UK.

German Rail Sales, c/o DTS Ltd, 18 Conduit Street, London W1R 9TD, UK. Tel: (0171) 290 1135.

Homelink International (Home Exchange Holidays), 84 Lees Gardens, Maidenhead, Berks SL6 4NT, UK. Tel: (01628) 31951.

Lufthansa, 23-26 Piccadilly, London W1V 0EJ, UK. Tel: (0171) 355 4994.

Lufthansa, 1st Floor, Concorde House, Trinity Park, Bickenhill Lane, Birmingham B37 7ES, UK. Tel: (0121) 767 2020.

Lufthansa, Grattan House, 68-72 Lower Mount Street, Dublin, Ireland. Tel: (01) 761595/6.

Lufthansa, Phoenix House, 78 St Vincent Street, Glasgow G2 5UB, UK. Tel: (0141) 2217132/3.

Lufthansa, 2nd Floor, Olympic House, Manchester International Airport, Manchester M22 5QX, UK. Tel: (0161) 493 2000.

MISCELLANEOUS ADDRESSES (IN GERMANY)

Aktion Sühnezeichen Friedensdienste e.V. (organisation for voluntary work), Postfach 154, D-10321 Berlin, Germany. Tel: (030) 55 19 03 10. Fax: (030) 55 19 03 76.

Allgemeiner Deutscher Fahrrad-Club e.V. (German Bicycle Club), Bundesgeschaftsstelle, Hollerallee 23, D-28209 Bremen, Germany. Tel: (0421) 346290. Fax: (0421) 3462950.

Arbeitsgemeinschaft der öffentlich-rechtlichen Rundfunkanstalten Deutschlands ARD (Association of Public Broadcasting Corporations), Arnulfplatz 42, D-80335 München, Germany.

Arbeitsgemeinschaft der Verbraucherverbände (Union of Consumer Associations), Heilsbachstr. 20, D-53123 Bonn, Germany. Tel: (0228) 6489-0. Fax: (0228) 644258.

Arbeitsgemeinschaft für Jugendhilfe (Youth Assistance Association), Haager Weg 44, D-53127 Bonn, Germany.

Arbeitsgemeinschaft Neuer Deutscher Film (New German Films Association), Agnerstr. 14, D-80789 München, Germany.

Arbeitskreis Freiwillige Soziale Dienste, Postfach 10 11 42, D-70010 Stuttgart, Germany. Tel: (0711) 2159-0. Fax: (0711) 2159-288.

Auskunftstelle für Postleitzahlen des Auslandes (information on international postcodes), Postfach 11 00, D-35035 Marburg, Germany. Tel: (06421) 966-435 or 966-436.

Bund für Umwelt und Naturschutz Deutschland e.V. (German Association for the protection of the environment and nature), Im Rheingarten 7, D-53225 Bonn, Germany. Tel: (0228) 400970. Fax: (0228) 4009740.

Bundesarbeitsgemeinschaft Jugendaufbauwerk (Federal Association for the Development of Youth Organisations), Haager Weg 44, D-53127 Bonn, Germany.

Baur-Versand (mail order company), Bahnhofstr. 10, D-96222 Burgkunstadt, Germany.

The British Bookshops GmbH, Börsenstr. 17, D-60313 Frankfurt, Germany. Tel: (069) 280492. Fax: (069) 287701.

Christlicher Friedensdienst e.V., (organisation for voluntary work),

Rendelerstr. 9-11, D-60385 Frankfurt, Germany. Tel: (069) 459072. Fax: (069) 461213.

Deutsch-Britische Juristenvereinigung e.v., (British-German Jurists Association), Generalsekretariat, Neuer Wall 42, D-20354 Hamburg, Germany. Tel: (04) 378687-11. Fax: (04) 8687-20.

Deutsche Bischofskonferenz (Catholic Church), Sekretariat, Kaiserstr. 163, D-53133 Bonn, Germany.

Deutsche Forschungsgemeinschaft, Referat III 0 6, Kennedyallee 40, Postfach 20 50 04, D-53175 Bonn, Germany. Tel: (0228) 8851. Fax: (0228) 885 2221.

Deutscher Akademischer Austauschdienst (German Academic Exchange Service), Jägerstr. 22-23, D-10117 Berlin, Germany. Tel: (030) 231208-0.

Deutscher Bundesjugendring (German Federal Youth Council), Haager Weg 44, D-53127 Bonn, Germany.

Deutscher Frauenrat (German Women's Council), Simrockstr. 5, D-53113 Bonn, Germany.

Evangelische Kirche in Deutschland (Protestant Church in Germany), Kirchenamt, Herrenhäuserstr. 12, D-30419 Hannover, Germany.

Grüne Liga e.V. (Green League), Friedrichstr. 165, D-10117 Berlin, Germany. Tel: (030) 2292990. Fax: (030) 2291822.

Naturschutzbund Deutschland e.V., Bundesgeschäftsstelle, Herbert-Rabius-Str. 26, D-53225 Bonn. Tel: (0228) 975610. Fax: (0228) 9756190.

Otto Versand (mail order catalogue), Bestellservice, D-20088 Hamburg, Germany.

RTL (Television Channel), Aachener Str. 1036, D-50858 Köln, Germany.

SAT.1 (Satellite Television), Otto-Schott-Str. 13, D-55127 Mainz, Germany.

Stiftung Warentest (Consumer Goods Testing Foundation), Lützowplatz 11-13, D-10785 Berlin, Germany. Tel: (031) 2631-0. Information helpline: (03) 0 2623014.

Unweltbundesamt (Federal Environmental Agency), Bismarckplatz 1, D-13585 Berlin, Germany.

Verein English Theatre e.V., Kaiserstr. 52, D-60329 Frankfurt, Germany. Tel: (069) 2423160.

Verkehrsclub Deutschland e.V., Eifelstr. 2, D-5311 Bonn, Germany. Tel: (0228) 985850. Fax: (0228) 444290.

Zentralrat der Juden in Deutschland (Central Council of the Jews in Germany), Rüngsdorfer Str. 6, D-53173 Bonn, Germany.

Zentrale Auskunftstelle für den Auslandspostdienst, Postfach 10 00 00, D-60285 Frankfurt, Germany. Tel: (0130) 804141.

Zweites Deutsches Fernsehen ZDF (TV Channel 2), Postfach 4040, D-55100 Mainz, Germany.

MISCELLANEOUS ADDRESSES (IN THE UK)

Association Internationale des Etudiants en Sciences Economiques et Commerciales (AIESEC), 2nd Floor, 29-31 Cowper Street, London EC2A 4AP, UK. Tel: (0171) 336 7939. Fax: (0171) 336 7971.

The British Institute of International and Comparative Law, Charles Clore House, 17 Russell Square, London WC1B 5DR, UK. Tel: (0171) 636 5802.

The Central Bureau, 16 Malone Road, Belfast BT9 5BN, UK. Tel: (01232) 664418.

The Central Bureau, 3 Bruntsfield Crescent, Edinburgh EH10 4HD, UK. Tel: (0131) 447 8022.

The Central Bureau, Seymour Mews House, Seymour Mews, London W1H 9PE, UK. Tel: (0171) 486 5101.

Community Action Programme for Education and Training for Technology (Comett), Sanctuary Buildings, Great Smith Street, London SW1P 3BT, UK. Tel: (0171) 925 5254. Fax: (0171) 935 5379.

Contributions Agency, Department of Social Security, Overseas Contributions, Longbenton, Newcastle NE98 1YX, UK. Tel: (0191) 2135000.

Department of Trade and Industry, Ashdown House, 123 Victoria Street, London SW1E 6RB. Tel: (0171) 2155354. Fax: (0171) 2155989.

Deutscher Akademischer Austauschdienst (German Academic Exchange Service), 17 Bloomsbury Square, London WC1A 2LP. Tel: (0171) 4044065. Fax: (0171) 4302634.

German Historical Institute, 17 Bloomsbury Square, London WC1A 2LP. Tel: (0171) 4045486.

German Film Library, Viscom Ltd, Unit B11, Parkhall Road Trading Estate, London SE21 8EL. Tel: (0181) 7614015.

King Edward VII British-German Foundation, 23 Falcondale Road, Westbury on Trym, Bristol BS9 3JS. Tel: (01117) 9623613.

MISCELLANEOUS ADDRESSES (IN OTHER COUNTRIES)

Headhunters Guides, Avotek Publishers, PO Box 38141, NL-6503 AC Nijmegen, Netherlands. Tel: (08894) 50502. Fax: (08894) 50769.

Index

accommodation, 81
address, 143
advertisements, 60, 83
adult education, 130
agriculture, 17, 30
airport, 19
Anglo-German Association, 35
Angst, 45
animals, 44
application letters, 63
Arbeitsamt, 57
au pair, 67
automotive industry, 17, 26

Baden-Württemberg, 17
banking, 31, 78
Bayern (Bavaria), 17
Blue Angel, 137
beach towels, 41
Berlin, 18
Brandenburg, 18
Bremen, 18
breweries, 20
business, 140
Bundesländer, 17
BWS Germanlingua, 49

catholics, 21
card games, 103
car   (buying), 134
       (driving), 133
car (manufacturing), 17, 26
carnival, 114
CESA, 53, 55
chambers of commerce, 151
charities, 44
chemical industry, 27, 28
Christians, 23
Christmas, 113
church, 21
church tax, 78
class system, 42
clothing, 42
Climate, 23
colleges, 124, 128
cookery, 104
colleagues, 93
communication technology, 19, 28

commuting, 132
contraception, 100
contract
       (rental), 85
       (employment), 90
conversation, 140
correspondence courses, 130
customs and traditions, 113
CV, 66
cycling, 132

DID, 48, 55
directory enquiries, 142
drinks, 108

East Germany, 25, 132
eating, 44, 104
eating out, 107
economic miracle, 11
electrical industry, 18, 26, 28
emergency numbers, 142
employment, 57
employment agencies, 59
engineering, 17, 26, 28
entertaining, 112
environment, 26, 29, 43

fast food, 107
fishery, 19, 30
flat-hunting, 81
food consumption, 44
food production, 20, 29
food purchasing, 97
forestry 18, 30
friends, 102
furniture, 86

geography, 17
German language, 48
Green Dot, 137
gifts, 43, 112
Goethe-Institut, 35, 53, 55
Grundgesetz, 11, 25

Hamburg, 18
Headhunters/Avotek, 59
healthcare, 76, 97
Hessen (Hesse), 19
hobbies, 44, 103

household equipment, 87
Horizonte, 49, 55
humour, 39

immunisation, 77
Industry, 17
insurance, 77

Jewish communities, 23
job hunting, 57

Kapito, 49, 55
Kindergarten, 122
knitting, 44

Länder, 17
language, 48
law, 11
letter writing, 143
litter disposal, 135
living standard, 11

magazines, 115
mail order, 100
Mecklenburg-Westpommern (Mecklenburg-
 Western Pomerania), 19
mining, 19, 29
Muslims, 23

Niedersachsen (Lower Saxony), 19
newspapers, 60, 115
Nordrhein-Westfalen (North Rhine
 Westfalia), 20

optical instruments, 19, 21, 29
Ordnungsliebe, 45
Overseas Placing Unit, 58
overseas trade, 18

pacifism, 42
personal hygiene, 45
Pharmaceutical industry, 18, 27
Politics, 12
postal rates, 148
postcodes, 143
post office, 146
Protestants, 23
ports, 18
prejudice, 38, 39
primary school, 122
public transport, 32, 132
Publishing, 21, 33
punctuality, 149

queueing, 46

racism, 38
railway, 32, 132
recipes, 104
registration, 74

religion, 23
rent, 81
residence permits, 73
restaurants, 109
Rheinland-Pfalz (Rhineland-Palatinate), 20

Saarland, 20
Sachsen (Saxony), 20
Sachsen-Anhalt (Saxony-Anhalt), 21
salary, 90
Schleswig-Holstein, 21
schools, 122
self employment, 60
shipbuilding, 19, 21
shopping, 96
shop opening hours, 96
social security, 11, 75
steel industry 18, 27, 29
Stiftung Warentest, 101

tax, 78
telephoning, 140
textile industry, 18, 29
titles, 143
Thüringen (Thuringia), 21
tourism, 18, 32
toys, 43
trade fairs, 151
trade unions, 91
training, 129
transport, 32, 132
travel, 36, 132
Treuhandanstalt, 26
Trust Agency, 26

unification, 25
universities, 51, 127
university summer schools, 51

vacation work, 69
vegetarian food, 44
vineyards, 17, 20, 37
visas, 73
visiting, 112
vocational training, 129
voluntary work, 67

wages, 90
waste disposal, 135
waste management, 135
West Germany, 25
wine drinking, 108
wine growing, 17, 20, 37
Wirtschaftswunder, 11, 25
women, 41
work experience, 50
work permits, 73

Zentralstelle für Arbeitsvermittlung, 57